I0813520

Have Horn, Will Travel

Junior Cook, circa 1986. Photo by David Spitzer.

Have Horn, Will Travel

The Life and Music of Herman "Junior" Cook

Courtney M. Nero

Number 21 in the North Texas Lives of Musicians Series

University of North Texas Press
Denton, Texas

Printed in the United States of America.

10 9 8 7 6 5 4 3 2 1

Permissions:
University of North Texas Press
1155 Union Circle #311336
Denton, TX 76203-5017

The paper used in this book meets the minimum requirements of the American National Standard for Permanence of Paper for Printed Library Materials, z39.48.1984. Binding materials have been chosen for durability.

Library of Congress Cataloging-in-Publication Data

Names: Nero, Courtney M., 1972- author
Title: Have horn, will travel : the life and music of Herman "Junior" Cook / Courtney M. Nero.
Other titles: North Texas lives of musicians series no. 21.
Description: Denton, Texas : University of North Texas Press, [2025] | Series: Number 21 in the North Texas lives of musicians series | Includes bibliographical references and index.
Identifiers: LCCN 2025036252 (print) | LCCN 2025036253 (ebook) | ISBN 9781574419825 cloth | ISBN 9781574419900 ebook
Subjects: LCSH: Cook, Junior | Saxophonists--United States--Biography | Jazz musicians--United States--Biography | LCGFT: Biographies
Classification: LCC ML419.C667 N47 2025 (print) | LCC ML419.C667 (ebook) | DDC 788.7/165092 [B]--dc23/eng/20250820
LC record available at https://lccn.loc.gov/2025036252
LC ebook record available at https://lccn.loc.gov/2025036253

Have Horn, Will Travel is Number 21 in the North Texas Lives of Musicians Series.

Parts of this book were previously printed in Courtney M. Nero, "Junior Cook: Quintessential NYC Hard-Bop Tenor," *Jazz Journal* (UK), 15 July 2023, https://jazzjournal.co.uk/2023/07/15/junior-cook-quintessential-hard-bop-tenor/.

The electronic edition of this book was made possible by the support of the Vick Family Foundation.

On the cover: Junior Cook, circa 1986. Photo by David Spitzer.

Typeset by vPrompt eServices.

To my mom, Lorraine C. Nero,
for your love.

To my dad, the late James H. Nero Sr.,
for your unfailing confidence.

To my Aunt B.,
for Pres.

To cousin Elizabeth,
for Moore's Love and Peace.

To Denise and David,
Always there.

To Naomi, Asa, and Reagan,
The bee's knees. Keep doing great things.
I love you more than I can express.

To my wife Sabrina,
I dream a dream, and she is you.

Contents

Introduction

Rob Bamberger, host of the *Hot Jazz Saturday Night* program on American University's WAMU-FM radio (Washington, DC), affirmed years ago in a radio ad for his show that a love for jazz "doesn't start with scholarship, it starts with discovery." My introduction to Herman "Junior" Cook followed that pattern. Around 1992 my college friend and fellow jazzhead, guitarist Alex Goldelman, let me borrow the Harper Brothers' (drummer Winard Harper and trumpeter Phillip Harper) compact disc release *Remembrance: Live at the Village Vanguard* (Verve Records, 1990), which featured a cover arrangement of Horace Silver's composition "Kiss Me Right." The tune's catchy melody and chord changes drew me in. I later bought Silver's *Doin' the Thing: The Horace Silver Quintet at the Village Gate* (Blue Note, 1961) on compact disc, curious to hear how the original recording of "Kiss Me Right" differed from the Harper Brothers' cover; Silver's original cut was swinging even harder.

Saxophonist Herman "Junior" Cook, featured on that Silver album, was saying something. His deliberate phrasing and his confident tone captivated me. I discovered that many of Silver's hits, epistles in the canon of jazz music, featured Cook in the quintet's front line along with trumpeter Richard Allen "Blue" Mitchell (13 March 1930–21 May 1979).

Fast forward almost twenty years, and I dedicated some of my newly found free time to researching Cook's life and music while on a society-wide COVID-19 lockdown. I was dismayed that I found very little information. Thus, if this research effort can be said to have followed any methodology, it was one of connecting the dots. I unearthed new information on his life and career where possible, but my second, just as important, goal was to consolidate extant information, properly sourced, in one volume for ease of reference to present the life and musical career of Junior Cook.

Another reason propelling this work is a certain disdain toward the phrase "unsung hero," in reference to a jazz musician: lesser known, obscure, forgotten, overlooked. The phrase usually implies that there are only so many top spots available in the jazz pantheon: "Well . . . we've already put Bird and Trane and Getz and Woods and Mulligan on this pedestal. No room left." Ben Ratliff, in an article on John Coltrane for the *Washington Post*, put it this way: "So much of American culture for so long has been based on great works. Maybe it's a question of standards or simply a measure of saving time. The questions often come down to: Who owns the crown? (One of the posthumous Coltrane reissue projects, from the 1990s, was titled *The Heavyweight Champion.*)"[1]

As if on cue, as this draft was coming to completion, I heard a retrospective on the career of Steven Sondheim on National Public Radio (NPR) (11 January 2024), in which critic Bob Mondello escorted Sondheim to the "genius pantheon."[2] The phrase "unsung hero" is akin to "honorable mention" in the jazz world. Ratliff asserts (correctly, in this author's view) that jazz "does not comply" with the great-works model, precisely because it "is always going somewhere in real time."[3] This work aims to trace where Junior Cook came from and where his musical journey took him, because I contend that his journey is worth retracing.

I discovered little "a-ha" moments during the research, passing data points that enhanced the significance of Junior Cook's storyline for me personally. For example, Cook first met pianist Horace Silver in my beloved Washington, DC, when the two found themselves in the city gigging and sitting in with saxophonist Lou Donaldson. This meeting eventually sparked an association that, within a year or so, kicked off one of the best bands in the history of jazz, the Horace Silver Quintet of 1958–1964, which featured leader Silver (piano), Mitchell (trumpet), Cook (tenor saxophone), Gene Taylor (bass), and Louis Hayes and Roy Brooks (drums). Also, be it coincidence or the ultimate mark of the sympatico that they shared in music and in life, Cook and his latter-day quintet partner, trumpeter Bill Hardman, both died at age 57, although in different years (1992 and 1990, respectively).

The stories in this work are true to the best of the collective memory of those who contributed. It might be called a biographical memoir, if there were such a thing. I never had the privilege of meeting Junior Cook personally. The stories that form this account of his life, living, and career have been gathered in oral or written interviews with musicians, friends, and associates of Cook, a few interviews (radio, press) with Cook himself, liner notes, and other resources. Cook's attitudes, feelings, and interpretations are those that he relayed to his friends and fellow musicians, who, in turn, relayed them to me. I have worked diligently to properly attribute Cook's attitudes and those of his friends and associates.

I appreciate those whose contributions, stories, anecdotes, and very personal details made this project possible (see the acknowledgments). I take sole ownership of any mistakes or inaccuracies, while also acknowledging the challenge of chronicling Cook's musical career some thirty years after his death, navigating through the partial fog of memories of events some forty-plus years in the past. I also appreciate pianist Wade Beach, who sparked my interest and love of jazz biographies.

As a jazz musician and saxophonist, this project was one of duty. This work responds to LeRoi Jones (Amiri Baraka) and his call, in the introduction of his *Blues People: Negro Music in White America*, to document our people and our music:

> There is yet much work to be done to properly bring the music into the open light of international understanding and collective social development and use . . . the widespread and routine scholarly and artistic institutionalization of the music is still very limited. It needs not only to further illuminate the obscure history, but to bring all the voices, the contributors, the pioneers, the innovators, the unknown and little-known facts and people, up front where they belong. The actual stages and dimensions of the music's development—how and where and why and by whom and with what historical impact—must still be reconstructed. The specific music of the various regions and cities has to be studied more closely. And with the social and economic and institutional stability with which European "classical" music is studied.[4]

Perhaps other musicians and scholars will take up Baraka's charge and research the lives and careers of other saxophone greats: Jane Ira Bloom, Tina Brooks, Joe Henderson, Steve Lacy, Yusef Lateef, Warne Marsh, Branford Marsalis, Bennie Maupin, Hank Mobley, Vi Redd, Sam Rivers, Charlie Rouse, Stanley Turrentine, Grover Washington Jr., and so many others.

My aim is to ensure that saxophonist Junior Cook's name will no longer share the same space with that hackneyed phrase "unsung hero." This book sings. It sings of Herman "Junior" Cook.

Chapter 1

Pensacola-Born and Early Years

Yes, indeed! Hey, you got my full credentials there. Yes.
—Herman "Junior" Cook, September 1988[1]

Pensacola-Born

Herman "Junior" Cook is the Cornell West of the tenor saxophone. His playing is confident, learned, well-spoken, eloquent. His phrases and logic sometimes catch listeners off guard and they find themselves hanging on his every utterance. Junior Cook does not beg. He doesn't play tricks. He needs neither your approval nor your validation. His melodies are self-validating, rooted in bluesy bop excellence, born and raised in the South, formed on the road and molded in New York, and destined for some of jazz history's great bands. While many musicians race along, flashing their technique like a gilded badge, Junior Cook's saxophone says, "Walk with me; come let us reason together."

Herman Columbus Cook was born on 22 July 1934 in Pensacola, Florida, to Joseph Lath Cook (1886–1975) and Mary C. Gilliam Cook (1897–1965).[2] Cook's siblings included Josie Mae Cook (Echo) (1917–1985), Robert Lath Cook (1924–2001), and John Lee Cook (1927–2000). The US Federal

LOCATION: Street (1)	House number (2)	HOUSEHOLD DATA: Number of household (3)	Home owned or rented (4)	Value of home or monthly rental (5)	Farm (6)	NAME (7)	RELATION (8)	CODE (A)	Sex (9)	Color or race (10)	Age at last birthday (11)	Marital status (12)	EDUCATION: Attended school (13)	Highest grade completed (14)	CODE (B)	PLACE OF BIRTH (15)	CODE (C)	CITIZENSHIP (16)	RESIDENCE: City, town, or village (17)	County (18)
Brainard	413	344	R	9	No	McDonald, Tommy	Head	0	M	Neg	40	M	No	4	4	Georgia	78		Pensacola	Escambia
						Evelina (x)	wife	1	F	Neg	34	M	No	6	6	Louisiana	85		Pensacola	Escambia
						Stella	daughter	2	F	Neg	15	S	Yes	8	8	Florida	79		Pensacola	Escambia
	415	350	R	9	No	Cook, Joseph L.	Head	0	M	Neg	52	M	No		90	Alabama	82		Pensacola	Escambia
						Mary (x)	wife	1	F	Neg	42	M	No	8	8	Florida	79		Pensacola	Escambia
						Robert	son	2	M	Neg	15	S	Yes	H2	10	Florida	79		Pensacola	Escambia
						John L.	son	2	M	Neg	8	S	Yes	1	1	Florida	79		Pensacola	Escambia
						Herman	son	2	M	Neg	5	S	No			Florida	79			

US Federal Census record of the Cook family, 1940.

Census in 1940 listed Cook's family as follows: John L. Cook, age 52; Mary Cook, age 42; Robert Cook, age 15; John L. Cook, age 8; and Herman Cook, age 5.[3] (The 1940 Federal Census record separately listed Josie M. Echo [nee Cook], Cook's older sibling, who was in her mid-20s at that time. She married Alexander (Aleck) Echo in the late 1940s or early 1950s and resided at 504 East Lloyd, Pensacola, Florida.)[4] The young Cook likely took his middle name from his paternal grandfather, Columbus Cook.

Cook was born into a musical family; both his father and older brother Robert played trumpet in the local "territory" bands of the day, and his brother John sang.[5] Eric Cook, great-nephew of Herman Cook, underscored the musical lineage, noting that most all the family was involved in music in some form, but Cook ("Uncle Herman") was the one who made a career out of it.[6] Young Herman Cook nurtured other talents briefly; at 12 years old he was recognized with honorable mention in the *Pensacola News Journal* as a "good cartoonist."[7] In a 1958 questionnaire for Leonard Feather's *Encyclopedia of Jazz*, Cook cited his father and brother as musical influences. He also noted that he had always loved music and "never have been anything or wanted to be anything else" other than a musician.[8]

Cook's early childhood home was located at 415 East Brainerd Street in Pensacola, according to census data.[9] East Brainerd Street placed Cook's home within Pensacola's Eastside neighborhood, located northeast of downtown. African Americans, previously restricted to Pensacola's Westside community, settled in Eastside in the early 1940s when the neighborhood was integrated. Pastors, doctors, and educators moved to the area, which was bordered by Cervantes Street to the south, Ninth Avenue to the west, Hayne Street to the east (presently overshadowed by Interstate Route 110), and Leonard Street to the north.

The matriarch Mary Cook died in mid-1965; the death notice listed her residence as 1009 N. Davis Street (now Davis Highway), around the corner and two blocks south of the Brainerd Street property, and cited Herman C. Cook as residing in Brooklyn, New York, at the time.[10] Cook's father died in early 1975, according to a *Pensacola News Journal* death notice. The death notice also listed Joseph L. Cook's surviving siblings at the time: "two sisters, Mrs. Lula Harris of Tuvern, Ala. and Mrs. Susie Norman of Cleveland,

Ohio; a brother, James Cook of New York." Funeral services for Joseph L. Cook took place at Zion Hope Primitive Baptist Church in Pensacola on February 7, 1975.[11]

Cook highlighted in a 1988 interview with radio host Leigh Kamman that Ray Sheppard ("Ray Shep") was his music teacher and provided his foundation on saxophone. Pensacola-born jazz saxophonist Joe Evans, in his autobiography (with Christopher Brooks), *Follow Your Heart*, highlighted the wide reach of clarinetist, saxophonist, bandleader, and school band instructor Sheppard as an instructor and influence on himself, Cook, and other Pensacola musicians. Sheppard succeeded trumpeter Joseph Jessie in Pensacola as the director of the Federal Music Project music program in Pensacola following Jessie's untimely murder at the hands of a student in 1936.[12] Ray Sheppard, an accomplished musician with one of the best local bands in the area, also was highly regarded as band instructor at Pensacola's Booker T. Washington High School, where Cook started on alto saxophone in 1948; he later switched to tenor saxophone.[13] A Pensacola City Directory listed Herman C. Cook, residing at 415 East Brainerd, as a student in 1952.[14] Booker T. Washington High School was a segregated school that opened in 1916. Ray Sheppard's instruction and preparation likely built a following among succeeding classes of young musicians who emerged from his tutelage to pursue music careers, including jazz altoists Evans and Gigi Gryce.

Teenage Herman showed early dedication to music. Jean Jones, a Pensacola resident who went to school with Cook's older brother John remembered that Herman was quiet and one who loved his music. She recalled that his brother Robert played trumpet or cornet and his brother John sang in the high school chorus and had a nice voice. Booker T. Washington High School in segregated Pensacola offered the city's African American students a fraction of the resources available to white students. Jones recalled the local elementary school for African Americans spanning first through sixth grades and the high school covering seventh through twelfth grades. The high school featured thirty-five, sometimes more than forty students in a class, but she emphasized that the students had much more respect for elders and for education at that time. According to Jones, Booker T. Washington Junior College,

Extra Extra Extra

RAY SHEP

MATINEES TUESDAYS AND THURSDAYS BEGINNING AT 7:30 AT ODD FELLOWS HALL

There will be Matinees at Odd Fellows Hall Every Tuesday P. M.—6:30 UNTIL—ADMISSION 15c

Managed by Odd Fellows and W. H. S. Athletic Asso'n

MUSIC BY RAY SHEP'S ORCHESTRA

Hall is air conditioned and comfortable. Hall is open to engagements at a low rental

Advertisement for performance by Ray Shep's Orchestra at Odd Fellows Hall, Pensacola, Florida. The ad was carried in a weekly Pensacola, Florida, publication, *The Colored Citizen*, 26 May 1939, vol. 26, no. 33, page 4. Image courtesy of the Digital Library of the University of West Florida, Pensacola.

STOP – LOOK – LISTEN

BO - BO EDWARDS AND HIS COLLEGIANS

200 E. GONZALEZ ST. — JANUARY 23

PLAYING EVERY

WEDNESDAY and FRIDAY

For Your Entertainment — Featuring

GERTRUDE JONES, the Girl with the Million Dollar Voice —— and our one and only BO-BO with his Guitar

TOM'S TAVERN

"The House of Fine Entertainment"

THOMAS (TOM) GOLSON, Prop.

Advertisement for live performance by "Bo-Bo" Edwards and His Collegians with vocalist Gertrude Jones at Tom's Tavern, Pensacola, Florida. The ad was carried in "The Colored Citizen," 29 August 1952, vol. 39, no. 16, page 2. Image courtesy of the Digital Library of the University of West Florida, Pensacola.

Picture of Raymond Sheppard from Booker T. Washington Senior High School Yearbook, 1965.

where she attended from 1952 to 1954 and Cook attended later in that decade, was co-located with Washington High School. Herman Cook dated Beulah Montgomery during his high school days, a "cute little girl," light-skinned ("yellow"), with long, wavy hair. Jones said some were sure they would eventually marry, but the music apparently set them apart once Cook departed Pensacola after high school to pursue his music career.[15]

Information is scarce on Cook's curriculum and instruction while at Booker T. Washington High School, but Sheppard's credentials and pedagogy are documented, as is Sheppard's success as a musician and his diligence in imparting quality music instruction to his students. Sheppard had been a classmate of swing bandleader Jimmie Lunceford while the two attended Fisk University.[16] Saxophonist Joe Evans characterized his lessons with Ray Shep as "very structured":

> Shep started out teaching me from a method book, probably a Carl Fischer instruction manual. One week I would focus on breathing or holding long tones. Another week there would be an exercise on articulation using the tongue for staccato passages. Shep frequently

> wrote these exercises himself in the style of contemporary popular tunes, like "Mule Face Blues" or "Up a Lazy River." A particular treat for me was when he wrote short works for two saxophones and played the lead part. I would play the second part. Then we would reverse parts, with me playing the lead and him playing the second. The technical difficulties of these exercises were designed to strengthen my sight-reading skills and they did just that. Many of these pieces had a variety of arpeggios, sforzandos, staccatos, key changes, slurs, sixteenth and thirty-second notes, and the like. All of these things would sometimes be found in a single exercise. I must give credit for my strong sight-reading ability to Shep and those complex exercises that he wrote for my lessons.[17]

Harold "Fess" (short for "professor") Andrews (born 1916), also a Pensacola musician, remarked in an oral history on the structure and foundation of early childhood musical education. He said that most children started music instruction on piano or violin. He intimated that "swing" music or "ragtime" was considered "adult music" and noted his "grandmother would have had a fit" if he, as a child, had played ragtime. Children received their instructional grounding in classical music; in Andrews's words, "You stuck to that method . . . and the methodical things that were in your method." Andrews also recounted having taught Cook and Cook playing in his group, making note in a 1981 interview of Cook's success and having "gone to stardom," citing Cook's collaborations with trumpeter Blue Mitchell.[18]

Sheppard's impact on music in Pensacola and successive classes of students was summarized in media coverage of his retirement in 1966. The article listed Cook ("Herman Cook, saxophonist with Horace Silver's orchestra") as one of his former students. The article also noted that Sheppard's Booker T. Washington High School band was "the first Negro high school band to present a half-time football show at the Senior Bowl in Ladd Memorial Stadium in Mobile [Alabama] in 1952."[19] It is plausible that Cook may have participated in this college football performance in 1952, which would have aligned with his senior year at Washington High School.

Other Pensacola musicians, including multi-instrumentalist Joseph Herring and trombonist Jimmy Cox, described the high caliber of musicians and musicianship coming out of Pensacola schools. Herring, born in 1948, highlighted Emmett Leroy (E. L.) Thompson's highly regimented teaching style at Washington Junior High School, saying his instruction was "no nonsense," "classically oriented," and focused on sight reading and the "cycle of fourths and fifths." Thompson's instruction at the junior high level fed students into Raymond Sheppard's care at the high school level; Thompson, in fact, was a classmate of Cook in high school, according to Herring. Herring also recalled how Pensacola musicians would listen to the top hits of the time from national bands, transcribe charts with excellent musical notation penmanship, and play those charts for Pensacola functions.[20] Jimmy Cox asserted in an oral history interview in 1981 that most of the musicians in Pensacola were "reading musicians," owing to the quality of their instruction under Raymond Sheppard and others.[21] Saxophonist John Boller of Pensacola recalled playing "marching band" and "symphonic band music" at Washington High School under Sheppard's leadership.[22]

Cook also noted early encouragement he received from alto saxophonist and composer Gigi Gryce. In the questionnaire completed for Feather's *Encyclopedia of Jazz*, Cook acknowledged Gryce's encouragement and advice. Cook said that Gryce, in New York, had sent him music in Florida, presumably to practice and to get a feel for what was happening in the New York scene. Cook counted Gryce as a "good friend" and said that talking to him was "inspiring and educational."[23] Cook, in turn, seemed to pay it forward by investing in other musicians: saxophonist John Boller, four years Cook's junior, said that he and Cook were good friends, practiced together, and that Cook taught him a lot. (Cook was a senior at Washington High when Boller was a freshman.)[24]

Cook's own burgeoning career testified to Sheppard's credentials and the effectiveness of his teaching regimen. Cook was born into a musical family but only started saxophone in high school in 1948. Sheppard's instruction and Cook's own apparent discipline charted Cook's career course in relatively short order. Cook played in Sheppard's group, the Jumping at the Savoy band, and also played in another Pensacola band, the Fabulous Flamingoes, according to Joe Herring.[25] Within around five years of starting to play the saxophone, Cook was pursuing a musical career in New York City. Within ten years he was gigging in the Chitlin' Circuit, had recorded as a sideman on Blue Note Records, had joined jazz pianist Horace Silver's band, and, by summer 1958, had played the blossoming Newport Jazz Festival (which was established only four years earlier).[26]

Sheppard also played a role in institutionalizing quality band instruction across the state. He was an elected officer of the Florida Association of Band Directors in Negro Schools (FABD), and his high school band participated in the association's first clinic in 1941. The clinic included workshops on rehearsal techniques, instrumental sectionals, band rehearsals, lectures, and networking opportunities among the students and band directors.[27]

While Sheppard was molding a generation's musicians in the Pensacola area, the advent of organizations like the FABD and efforts to undergird the Works Progress Administration's (WPA) Federal Music Project (FMP) in African American communities would bear fruit through the many Florida-born musicians who went on to change and advance music in the jazz idiom during this same time period. Cohen and Fitzgerald cite the FMP as hitting its peak in 1936, employing some fifteen thousand musicians.[28] (Cook was born in 1934.) That said, music excellence likely did not begin and end with the WPA FMP but rather was built on top of traditions of musical excellence established by the likes of Ray Sheppard, E. L. Thompson, Joseph Jessie, and others, as well as the territory bands in which they participated. Pensacola-born Cook shares company with a number of Florida-born musicians of note:

- Ida Goodson (piano), b. 1909, Pensacola
- Joe Evans (alto saxophone), b. 1916, Pensacola
- Theodore "Fats" Navarro (trumpet), b. 1923, Key West
- Idrees Suleiman (born Leonard Graham) (trumpet), b. 1923, St. Petersburg
- Sam Jones (bass), b. 1924, Jacksonville
- George General "Gigi" Gryce Jr. (alto saxophone), b. 1925, Pensacola
- Donald Shirley (piano), b. 1927, born in Jamaica and raised in Pensacola
- Julian "Cannonball" Adderley (alto saxophone), b. 1928, Tampa
- Oscar Dennard (piano), b. 1928 in Memphis, Tennessee, and raised in St. Petersburg

- George "Buster" Cooper (trombone), b. 1929, St. Petersburg
- Ray Charles Robinson Sr. ("Ray Charles") (piano, vocal), b. 1930 in Albany, Georgia, raised in Greenville, Florida
- Richard Allen "Blue" Mitchell (trumpet), b. 1930, Miami
- Nat Adderley (trumpet, cornet), b. 1931, Tampa
- Doug Carn (piano, organ), b. 1948, St. Augustine)

Pensacola and West Florida Cultural Intersections

Located in Florida's panhandle along the Gulf of Mexico, Pensacola punched above its weight with a cosmopolitan feel born of the US military presence, tourism and trade, and its proximity to the jazz and cultural center of New Orleans. James R. McGovern summarized that Pensacola was "not a typical southern city," noting the influence of the port and the role of the military—particularly the rapid expansion of Pensacola's Naval Air Station (NAS)—in urbanizing the city without industrialization and establishing Pensacola as part of what he termed the "New South": "Pensacola acquired typical characteristics of industrialized cities; its population became mobile, heterogeneous, cosmopolitan, business minded, and secular. In addition to the military's role, technology and culture disseminated from the nation's great cities also contributed to Pensacola's increasingly urban identity."[29] Madeleine Hirsiger Carr highlighted Pensacola as a resort destination along with Miami, Fort Myers, Palm Beach, Orlando, and Jacksonville. In contrast with Miami's sixty-five hotels, which hosted 134,122 guests in 1937, "Pensacola, with just four hotels, managed to draw 90,000 visitors during the same year, attesting to its popularity as a North Florida destination."[30] Jean Jones affirmed in an interview that Pensacola was "not a country town."[31]

Cook and other Black Floridians of course would have been exposed to the influence of these socioeconomic dynamics, even if not taking part in them directly because of institutionalized racism and segregation. In other words, the influx of tourists may have buoyed demand for local band performances in the area, even if Cook and other Black musicians were not permitted in the hotels that housed some of these tourists. Saxophonist Joe Evans characterized

Pensacola as "relatively progressive" in the 1920s and 1930s, especially in comparison to surrounding towns in Alabama and Mississippi. Evans notably observed, as an apparent sign of this progress, that he had "only" heard about one lynching in Pensacola, likely in the 1920s, if not earlier.[32]

The US Department of Commerce census for the state of Florida documented Escambia County, Florida, where Pensacola is located, as the seventh most populous county in Florida in 1940. Escambia County's 1940 population of 74,667 residents outnumbered the 70,074 residents of Florida's Orange County, which includes the city of Orlando. By 1950 Orange County had outpaced Escambia County's residential base, but the latter remained among the top ten Florida counties by population.[33]

Top Ten Florida Counties by Population in 1950, US Department of Commerce

County	Preliminary Population Count, 1950	Major City in County
Dade	488,689	Miami
Duval	302,711	Jacksonville
Hillsborough	248,536	Tampa
Pinellas	157,639	Clearwater, St. Petersburg
Polk	122,801	Lakeland
Palm Beach	114,144	Palm Beach
Orange	114,114	Orlando
Escambia	111,241	Pensacola
Broward	83,318	Fort Lauderdale
Volusia	73,151	Daytona Beach

Source: "1950 Census of Population, Preliminary Counts. Population of Florida By Counties, April 1, 1950," Series PC-2, No. 9, dated 11 August 1950, https://www2.census.gov/library/publications/decennial/1950/pc-02/pc-2-09.pdf, accessed 22 June 2023.

Pensacola's relative popularity as a North Florida destination contradicts impressions of the city as a backwater that lacked a draw for national-level musicians and artists. Brian Case's liner notes for Cook's album *Pressure Cooker* (Affinity, 1977), for example, claimed that Cook's early influences came from records, including Sonny Stitt, Wardell Gray, Illinois Jacquet, Gene Ammons, and Charlie Parker, "since Pensacola was the boondocks as far as jazz was concerned." By contrast, a December 1937 article in the *Pittsburg Courier*, an African American newspaper, highlighted the visit of Edward Kennedy "Duke" Ellington and jazz singer Ivy (Ivie) Anderson to Pensacola, where they were hosted (separately) by both the National Orchestra Syndicate and the Afro-American Insurance Company.[34] McGovern wrote of dances in Pensacola clubs in the 1940s "with performers of the stature of Duke Ellington and [pianist and bandleader] Buddy Johnson."[35] Aaron Long, a classmate of Pensacola-born jazz saxophonist Gigi Gryce, relayed that "all of the big bands that ever played, from Louis Armstrong all the way to Cab Calloway and Duke Ellington, came to Pensacola to perform during the forties."[36] Joe Herring recalled experienced jazz and blues saxophonist Hank Crawford playing at the 506 Club.[37] Adderley and Joe Evans both also spoke of Florida's local, "territory" bands as well. Ben Ratliff, in his *Coltrane: The Story of a Sound*, affirmed that in the late 1940s, jazz was still popular and "reputable touring bands" were playing venues in many not-so-large cities: "Gary, Indiana; Dayton, Ohio; Bogalusa, Louisiana; Sewickley, Pennsylvania; Beckley, West Virginia; Inkster, Michigan; and Pensacola, Florida."[38] The accounts in aggregate suggest that Pensacola was not as "backwater" as Case asserted in his liner notes.

Pensacola was also one of several Southern stops on the Chitlin' Circuit, an archipelago of African American music venues that featured Black entertainers who were not permitted in segregated America to perform in whites-only establishments. The clubs and theaters also obviously served Black audiences who were not allowed in whites-only venues. Pensacola's Belmont-Devilliers District, known as The Blocks, included a number of Black-owned entertainment venues, including the Savoy (later named Abe's 506 Club), and served as a commercial hub for Black business in Pensacola. Other area venues included the Dreamland Ballroom (1930s and 1940s), Williams Hall, Cufion Park dance hall, the Devilliers Street United Service Organization (USO) club (this location was opened for Black military personnel who were refused service at USOs serving white military officers), Tom's Tavern, the Ranger's Bar, and the Elks Club.[39] Pensacola sat among other Chitlin' Circuit stops hugging the Gulf Coast, including New Orleans, Louisiana; Biloxi, Mississippi; Mobile, Alabama; and Tallahassee, Florida. Pensacola resident Jean Jones also recalled attending dances at the Fricker Recreation Center, at the intersection of A and Strong Streets in Pensacola, where they might hear Clarence Salter (Rev. Salter) and his Jump Five band from 7:30 to 9:00 pm for an admission price of fifteen cents. On Friday evenings they might hear live music at the Elks Club, at the corner of Wright and Coyle, after Friday football games at Legion Field.[40] Multi-instrumentalist Joe Herring recalled some of the professional Pensacola bands of the 1960s, including the Rounders, the house band for the 506 Club; the Dothan Sextet, the house band for Tom's Tavern; and of course the Fabulous Flamingos.[41]

Pensacola nurtured its own staple of musicians who raised the bar of musicianship in the city; Pensacola and its citizens were not dependent on touring bands from out of town to provide high-quality music. Some accounts mark as a turning point in Pensacola's musical history the relocation of Ned Wyer's Cornet Band and Orchestra (also known as Wyer's Creole Cornet Band or the Silver Cornet Band) from New Orleans to Pensacola as early as 1868, bringing their Creole background and musical-cultural capital with them eastward to the west Florida town.[42] R. D. Pierce's history of Pensacola, *DeVilliers*, cites Ned Wyer's band of Creole musicians as being "famous during the years of 1873–1930," just four years before Cook's birth.[43] Oral histories recount a multitude of musical talent native to Pensacola, including several saxophonists:

- Jimmy Cox remembered Charlie Bruton as "one of the finest saxophonists you ever heard, just as much as Johnny Hodges";[44] Bruton left Ray Sheppard's Midnight Owls orchestra for a job out of town, which allowed saxophonist Joe Evans to take his spot, according to Evans's autobiography
- Evans and Cox also mentioned tenor saxophonist Robert Willis
- Cox also cited Butsy Douglas (saxophone)
- Wally Mercer Sr.
- Joseph Herring highlighted John Boller, whom he described as "a hell of a sax player" and noted that Boller (on saxophone) also played in a group (unspecified) that had included Cook's brother Robert on trumpet;

Herring also called out Reverend Salter, C. J. Deveaux, and "Juke" as talented Pensacola area saxophonists; pianist Charles (Charlie) Callier Sr., who was close to Cook, taught Herring many jazz songs, including Clifford Brown compositions

- Emory "Bo-Bo" Edwards (guitar)[45]
- David Washington (trumpet, vocals)
- Danny Goodman (bass)
- Florida's oral history Florida Memory Project also includes saxophonist George Hawkins
- Herring also was a classmate of Robert Cook Jr. (son of Robert Cook Sr. and nephew of Herman Cook), who, Herring noted, played first-chair trumpet in school; Herring complimented the Cooks all around as a talented family
- Henry Hodges "Chick" Minor, who played piano at the Savoy club and hosted jam sessions at the club

Compensation for Pensacola's high-quality music was competitive. Herring noted that he could make $40 per night playing dances and other gigs with the Fabulous Flamingos, whereas his mother made $25 per week as a house cleaner.[46]

Cook cited saxophonist Wardell Gray (1921–1955) as an influence in interviews and other sources, including a 1959 interview while on tour in Europe, captured in the book *Jazz Me Blues*. Cook highlighted that his playing, as documented in recordings, was "much closer to that of Wardell Gray" than to Sonny Rollins and John Coltrane, saxophonists to whom he was often compared in the late 1950s.[47] Gray was born in Oklahoma before migrating to Detroit, Michigan. He eventually centered his musical life in the West Coast bebop scene of the 1940s. Gray's recording career spanned only eleven years: his first recordings and recorded solos date from 1944 until his death in 1955.[48] Flowing, clean, deliberate playing are attributes that Gray and Cook have in common, especially throughout Cook's association with Horace Silver and his post-Silver association with Silver quintet alumnus Blue Mitchell. Though their respective attacks are distinctive—Gray's a lighter, Lester Young approach against Cook's more brawny tone—their melodic sense and output are similar.

In the questionnaire for Feather's *Encyclopedia of Jazz* to the question, "Who has been your favorite artist on your instrument?" Cook answered, "Wardell Gray, Sonny Stitt & Rollins, Hank Mobley, John Coltrane, Clifford Jordan." To the question, "Who has been the most important influence in your field of work?" Cook answered, "Gray, Stitt, Rollins."[49] The answers are reflected in Cook's playing just as clearly as they are written in his own handwriting on the questionnaire: Gray's lyricism and Stitt's precision are on display in Cook's performances through much of his career.

The Big Apple

Cook departed Pensacola for New York City after high school in 1952, encouraged by friends to pursue a musical career there.[50] His introduction to the jazz capital of the world seems to have been a rough one. By Cook's account, he "literally starved for a while" trying to make it in New York. He took work unloading trucks to support himself.[51]

In time Cook landed a position with Willie Mabon's blues orchestra. Mabon's early and mid-1950s recordings paired his boogie-woogie piano and suave vocals with tenor saxophone accompaniment, including Ernest Cotton on "I Don't Know" (Chess); Fred Clark on "I'm Mad" (Chess); Charles Ferguson on "You're A Fool" (Chess); and a number of recordings from 1953 to 1956 with Herbert Robertson. Little information is available on Cook's tenure with Willie Mabon, other than noting that Cook toured with Mabon in Southern music venues.[52]

Cook's association with Chicago bluesman Mabon and the rhythm and blues scene fits an adapted chronology of jazz and pop music specifically among Black audiences. While many jazz histories generally place bebop, cool jazz, and hard bop as chronologically successive genres in the idiom, jazz producer Michael Cuscuna noted that "nobody gave a shit" about cool jazz in New York City, marking it as "California stuff" and highlighting an East-West divide that transcended music genres.[53] Jazz writer David Rosenthal also asserted that "in Black neighborhoods, cool jazz went virtually unnoticed."[54] Instead, Rosenthal highlights rhythm and blues groups that filled the gap: "The early fifties saw an extremely dynamic rhythm and blues scene take shape, including a succession of brilliant doo-wop combos like the Ravens, the Clovers, and the Orioles; a New Orleans school centering on Fats Domino, Professor Long Hair, Shirley and Lee, and others; urban blues of the Muddy Waters and Bobby Bland type; and much else besides. This music, and not cool jazz, was what chronologically separated bebop and hard bop."[55] The Great Migration, along with postwar prosperity, paved the way for Southern-bred blues musicians to gain popularity in Northern urban centers and for Northern Black audiences to use their resources to demand more of this music in wax and in live performances. Radio stations in metropolitan areas with substantial Black populations began to play more rhythm and blues. Chicago Blues, which included the likes of Mabon, often was comprised of electric guitar, harmonica, piano, bass, drums, and sometimes a saxophone "as a symbol of urban sophistication"[56]—a spot tailor-made for Cotton, Clark, Ferguson, Robertson, and Cook.

Cook took various sideman gigs in the early and mid-1950s, including with Mabon; the Dell Tones, a female vocal group; and bassist Gloria Bell. According to Cook in the liner notes for *Pressure Cooker*, he spent only a couple years in New York, feeling he wasn't ready for the New York scene. He reveled in the opportunity to see and hear his musical heroes in New York City, including at the famed Apollo Theater; the Apollo's daily shows toggled between music acts and movie shorts. Cook recounted spending a good part of the day at the Apollo, sneaking in a sandwich, napping during the movie shorts, and waking up to hear Sonny Stitt and the Earl Bostic band.

Cook by his own account grew tired of "starving" and "sleeping in other cats' rooms" in New York City, and at some point between 1952 and 1955 he returned to Pensacola. Cook enrolled at Washington Junior College in the mid-1950s, according to academic records currently housed at Pensacola State College and according to vocalist Timmy Shepherd's recollection of Cook's own retelling of his history.[57] Named for Booker T. Washington (same as Cook's Pensacola high school), Washington Junior College was the first junior college option for Blacks in still-segregated Florida. Pensacola Junior College (PJC) was established in 1948 and started with an enrollment of 136 students. (PJC was renamed Pensacola State College in 2010.)[58] Washington Junior College followed in 1949, the fifth public junior college in the state of Florida, the first Black junior college in Florida and first in the country, another apparent sign of the relative "progressiveness" of Pensacola in the deep South.[59] The Washington Junior College Bulletin for the 1955–1956 academic year recorded an enrollment of 93 freshman students.

Cook enrolled in three semesters of coursework at Washington Junior College from September 1955 through December 1956, according to his academic record. Cook's transcripts also document that he enrolled in two one-semester courses of Public School Music taught by H. L. Coleman, perhaps indicating that he had considered pursuing a career in education.

A 1957 Pensacola City Directory also listed a Herman C. Cook employed as an orderly at Pensacola's Baptist Hospital, listing his residence at the time as 1009 N. Davis, Pensacola, Florida.[60] As early as 1942, Alexander (Alex, Aleck) Echo, Cook's brother-in-law, was listed in the Pensacola City Directory as employed as an orderly at Baptist Hospital in Pensacola, possibly an "in" for Cook to have secured employment as well.[61]

With some junior college education and Pensacola employment under his belt, Cook departed Pensacola once more for another go at a music career in New York City circa 1957. A brief interview in 1985 published in the *Washington Post* cited Cook as "only recently" having arrived in New York from Pensacola at age 24 (his 24th birthday would have been in 1958) before he started attending rehearsals for Dizzy Gillespie's band.[62] In the 1958 questionnaire for Feather's *Encyclopedia of Jazz*, Cook listed his address as 1800 Seventh Avenue, New York, New York.[63]

Cook's pickup gigs continued with bassist Gloria Bell from June through December 1957, according to Cook's responses for Feather's *Encyclopedia of Jazz* questionnaire.[64] Separately, Cook also gigged with the Dell Tones (also known as the Delltones and the Dell-Tones). Entering the scene as the Enchanters in 1952, among the first female R&B groups, the Dell Tones—Frances Kelly, Della Simpson, and Gloria Lynne—held contracts in the 1950s with Brunswick (a subsidiary of Coral Records), Rainbow Records, and Baton Records, and maintained a schedule of live appearances under the management of the husband of singer Della Simpson. Shirley Bunny Foy replaced Gloria Lynne in the Dell Tones when the latter left the group for a solo career. Cook and trombonist Slide Hampton played in the Dell Tones

(Hampton arranged for the group), and Cook and Foy briefly were in a relationship. (Foy later traveled to Europe and remained there.) A Dell Tones gig at Washington, DC's Howard Theatre (discussed in the next chapter) was the coincidence that allowed Cook and Horace Silver to meet and play together for the first time.

What did Cook likely absorb from this chapter of his musical life? The Dell Tones classic early R&B sound was centered on a lead singer and background doo-wop vocals, often with a half or whole chorus of saxophone solo for spice, not unlike the Mabon blues formula. Though no recordings have been discovered to date of Cook in these groups, Cook likely honed his ability to speak (in a musical sense) succinctly in this R&B style and format. The Dell Tones' single "Little Short Daddy" (Rainbow 244, 1954) included R&B saxophone stalwart Clifford Scott, whose growling, muscular, jump-blues tenor sound, saxophone break-fills, and saxophone improvising over vocal background backing almost provides a blueprint of the Horace Silver hard bop instrumental hits to come, with Silver's own trademark breaks, fills, backgrounds, and shout choruses.

Cook's work in the rhythm and blues world may have contributed to his melodic sense. Pop (popular) music often hews closely to motifs built on close intervals (the distance between musical pitches). Descriptions of Cook's improvisational approach as melodic, flowing, and lyrical seem to imply his attention to a style not necessarily limited to diatonic movement but biased toward diatonic and intervallic movements of smaller distances. This approach might be contrasted with the likes of jazz saxophonists Charlie Rouse, Oliver Nelson, or, at an arguable extreme, Eric Dolphy, who displayed more angular, leaping approaches to improvisation marked by larger intervallic movements.

Cook also may have begun during this early period to build a durable, lasting sense of community among circles of musicians that would span his career. Cook, as examples later in the book will highlight, seemed to thrive on relationships and personal connections with like-minded musicians. This may have influenced his band associations; he moved far less frequently among bands—Horace Silver (1958–1964), Blue Mitchell (1964–1968/69), Bill Hardman (1978–1988)—possibly eager to build

DISTRICT THEATRES
NO. 7-3000

HOWARD 7th & T Sts. N.W.
Doors open at 12 noon
Stage: AL JEFFERONS SHOW: The Dells, Jimmy Reed, Screaming Jay Hawkins, The Nutmegs, The Dell-Tones, Margie Day, Andre Williams.
Screen: "WOMAN OF PITCAIRN ISLAND." Lynn Bari.

[illegible] 1215 You St., N.W.

Ad from *The Washington Post*, 22 April 1957, for entertainment at the Howard Theatre in Washington, DC. The advertised show includes "The Dells, Jimmy Reed, Screaming Jay Hawkins, the Nutmegs, The Dell-Tones, Margie Day, and Andre Williams." This may have been the Dell Tones' performance at the Howard Theatre that brought Cook to Washington, DC, and set the stage for his first introduction to Horace Silver.

and nurture relationships within a single group. Cook worked with Slide Hampton in the Dell Tones and, in later years, would again collaborate with him: the two were part of the personnel roster on Eddie Jefferson's album *The Main Man* (Inner City, 1977), and on Cook's own album *Good Cookin'* (Muse, 1980). Hampton, at Cook's request, composed a song for the *Good Cookin'* album based on the changes of John Coltrane's "Lazy Bird." Hampton's composition, "J.C.," carried double meaning, as the initials both for John Coltrane and Junior Cook. Louis Hayes and Cook connected for a year in the Horace Silver quintet (1958–1959) before Hayes left the Silver group for Cannonball Adderley's band; Hayes and Cook then reunited in the mid-1970s to form a quintet. After his six-year stint with Horace Silver's quintet, Cook reunited with Silver for the latter's 1988 release, *Music to Ease Your Disease* (Silverto). Cook and Mitchell, both alums of Silver's band from 1958 to 1964, continued to carry the torch, fronting a quintet with Mitchell as leader for another five years in the mid- to late-1960s.

Cook first recorded with pianist Mickey Tucker on Tucker's 1977 album, *Sojourn* (Xanadu). Their musical camaraderie extended effectively to the end of Cook's life; Tucker's piano supported the Bill Hardman–Junior Cook Quintet in the 1980s, Cook visited and gigged with Tucker following Tucker's relocation to Australia, and Tucker also played piano for Junior Cook's SteepleChase record releases in the late 1980s and 1990s before Cook's death in 1992. Drummer Leroy Williams also shared in this close-knit musical circle, contributing to the Hardman-Cook quintet and Cook's SteepleChase releases *On a Misty Night* (1989) and *The Place to Be* (1988).

Early 1958 found Cook rehearsing with Dizzy Gillespie's band at Dizzy's house in Corona, Long Island. Bassist Sam Jones introduced Cook and brought him to the rehearsal; Cook, in a 1985 interview, touted his friendship with Jones as part of the Florida fraternity of musicians who looked out for one another, Jones having been born in Jacksonville. No doubt, Cook's affiliation with Gillespie, one of jazz music's greatest icons, however brief, may have opened musical opportunities for Cook that were elusive during his first trip to New York City in the early 1950s. With James Moody—whom Cook cited as his "favorite saxophonist" in a 1985 interview—and Sonny Stitt flanking him in the reed section, Cook recalled a feeling of "sheer terror" and apparent self-doubt, mirroring his first stint in New York City in the early 1950s.[65] He tried to play softly so that any mistakes he made would be less noticeable—a story he relayed a few times over. In response, Dizzy encouraged him to play loud ("If you're going to make a mistake, make a big fat one! Then we'll know what to work on").[66] Cook reported working with Dizzy Gillespie's "combo" in March and April of 1958 and also said that he participated in a radio broadcast with Gillespie's combo during that time, according to Feather's *Encyclopedia* questionnaire.[67]

"Junior" appears to have been born during this time. Cook himself noted generically in a 1959 interview that people nicknamed him Junior because he often played with older musicians early in his music career.[68] In a 1991 press interview, Cook said that the nickname dated from his earliest arrival in New York. At age 18 (circa 1952), he said that he was often "the youngest one in the band" and the musicians "just started calling

[him] Junior."[69] Another story, from Cook's 1980s right-hand man, vocalist Timmy Shepherd, adds context to the nickname's staying power. Having concluded in his mind that he wasn't up to the job of holding a spot in the Gillespie band, the diffident Cook had packed his bag at a local hotel and sought to skip out. Saxophonist and flautist Frank Wess caught him as he was trying to leave: "Where you going, junior?" When Cook explained that he had planned to depart, Wess encouraged Cook that Dizzy would not have hired him if he (Dizzy) didn't think Cook was ready. "Go on back upstairs, junior," Wess instructed.

Cook in 1977 looked back on his first years in New York, recalling it as a tough time mentally and emotionally to thrust himself into the scene and to claim a position to grow and get gigs. In an appreciation for Horace Silver in *Radio Free Jazz*, he relayed, "Horace was helpful, encouraging. The group [Silver's quintet] was like a family. At that point in my career I was a very super-sensitive guy anyway and it took a whole lot of people almost to drag me literally and push to even go and get in his way [i.e., to approach Silver about taking him up on the offer to join his band]; so if he made me feel at ease behind that, he had to be cool."[70]

Within a year or so, Cook participated in a recording session for Kenny Burrell's *Blue Lights* album (Blue Note, recorded May 1958), which listed him in the liner notes' personnel roster as Junior Cook. Cook's several subsequent recordings as sideman and, eventually, as leader followed suit. Cook relayed years later, "When they put it [the nickname "Junior"] on the record label, it stuck."[71] Adopting a nickname fit the mold of the times, as it seemed commonplace for musicians: "Tina" Brooks (Harold Floyd Brooks, tenor saxophone); "Jaki" Byard (John Arthur Byard, piano, saxophone); "Duke" Ellington (Edward Kennedy Ellington, piano, bandleader); "Dizzy" Gillespie (John Birks Gillespie, trumpet); "Tubby" Hayes (Edward Brian Hayes, British multi-instrumentalist); "Buck" Hill (Roger Hill, tenor saxophone); "Duke" Jordan (Irving Sidney Jordan, piano); "Blue" Mitchell (Richard Allen Mitchell, trumpet); "Fats" Navarro (Theodore Navarro, trumpet); "Fathead" Newman (David Newman, tenor saxophone); "Vi" Redd (Elvira Redd, alto saxophone); and "Lucky" Thompson (Eli Thompson, tenor and soprano saxophones).

So started Cook's recording career. The Burrell album was Cook's first appearance on Blue Note Records. *Blue Lights* also appears to be the first recording of Cook's career, as there are no documented recording appearances for Cook with Mabon, Gloria Bell, the Dell Tones, Chris Powell and his Blue Flames, or with the Gillespie band.[72] A Blue Note promotional in *DownBeat* magazine, highlighting Burrell's release, announced "new tenor stars Junior Cook and Tina Brooks."[73] A review of *Blue Lights* a few years later noted overall that the soloists "acquit themselves with valor" and highlighted the young tenors: "Cook and Brooks make for interesting contrast as they alternate solos on 'Rock' and 'Chuckin'.' Though both men have similar approaches and are among the best of the younger crop of tenorists, there are many subtleties in their individual playing that serve to heighten the interest of the listener."[74] Burrell himself called Cook and Tina Brooks both his "unsung heroes" on tenor.[75] H. A. Woodfin, on the other hand, claimed in *Jazz Review* in 1959 that "Cook and Brooks are almost indistinguishable" on Burrell's album, descending "roughly from [Lester] Young, by [Dexter] Gordon, [Sonny] Stitt, [John] Coltrane, [Wardell] Gray, and God-knows-who else."[76]

Chapter 2

Fronting Silver

Right now I'd like to take a minute out, if I may, to introduce you to the group . . . a brand-new group, practically a brand-new group. First of all, we'd like to have you meet a very wonderful tenor saxophonist from Pensacola, Florida—Junior Cook.

—Horace Silver[1]

Fronting Silver

Cook is recognized most often for his tenure with the quintet of jazz pianist Horace Silver. While this book aims precisely to expand the reader's understanding of the whole of Cook's career and not to boil the entirety of Junior Cook down to "Sister Sadie," "Cookin' at the Continental," and "Tokyo Blues" (just a few of Silver's popular compositions), the period of Cook's musical career with Silver was indeed a significant one—one that marked the careers of both men indelibly. Silver found in Cook a reliable funk swinger to build his musical vision. Cook, in Silver's group, found a steady palette of compositions to interpret and a band that caught and kept the ear of the industry, spreading Cook's tenor sound far and wide in the jazz world.

Cook and Silver's paths first crossed in Washington, DC, in 1957. Cook was on a gig with the Dell Tones at the Howard Theatre in Washington, DC, as detailed in the previous chapter. Silver had traveled there to check out the scene following a gig in either Baltimore, Maryland, or Wildwood, New Jersey.[2] Silver remarked that Cook's playing came "as a great surprise" and impressed him when they both sat in with Lou Donaldson at a gig in Washington, DC, likely at Abarts Internationale jazz club at 1928 Ninth Street NW.[3] (Donaldson, circa spring 1957, had an "extended stay" gigging at Abarts, backed by a "house trio" of William "Keter" Betts on bass, Charles "Dolo" Coker on piano, and Grassella Oliphant, the music director at Abarts, on drums.[4]) Silver, later in 1957 or early 1958, called Cook to sub for tenor saxman Clifford Jordan for a week when Jordan took a leave to travel to California because of an illness in his family.[5] Cook also recounted that, once he became acquainted with Silver in DC, he jammed with Silver often in New York City and became very familiar with Silver's compositions, even before joining Silver's quintet.[6] Cook remained with the Gillespie band until the leader embarked on a European tour, possibly as part of Norman Granz's Jazz at the Philharmonic. Silver recounted eagerly that when Gillespie went overseas, "I grabbed him [Cook], and he's been with us since then."[7]

By 1958 Cook had secured a spot in Silver's quintet and a place in jazz history as sideman to one of jazz's iconic bands. The Silver quintet's performance at the Newport Jazz Festival on 6 July 1958 may be the earliest recording of Cook with the band. The recording of the quintet's performance was released in 2007/2008 as *Live at Newport '58* on Blue Note Records. Louis Smith (trumpet) shared the front line with Cook on the release; trumpeter Blue Mitchell joined the quintet later in 1958.

Video footage of the Horace Silver quintet in 1959 shows Cook likely on the Selmer Mark VI tenor saxophone that carried him through his career. The video also shows Cook playing a metal Otto Link mouthpiece, with its distinctive ligature and trademark ridge on the top. Cook later exchanged his Link for a hard rubber Meyer mouthpiece.[8]

One cannot avoid Cook's place in the genealogy of hard bop tenor saxophonists succeeding tenor saxophone master Hank Mobley. Though Cook directly followed tenorist Clifford Jordan in Horace Silver's quintet,

Hank Mobley (who proceeded Jordan) had a longer tenure as a front man in Silver's group, from 1954's *Horace Silver and the Jazz Messengers* to *The Stylings of Silver* in 1957 (both Blue Note). Aaron Gilbreath records that when Mobley was arrested, Clifford Jordan became Horace Silver's tenor saxophone player. Jordan's time in Silver's band was brief, however, and Junior Cook took the tenor saxophone spot when Jordan left the band.[9] Cook noted in an interview that Silver likely had "heard a little Hank Mobley influence in me" and that that sound may have sparked Silver's interest, given that Silver and Mobley had worked to great effect earlier in the original Jazz Messengers outfit with drummer Art Blakey. Cook concluded, "That's how the gig [with Silver] came about."[10]

And what *did* Cook walk into in Silver's quintet? No less than a cultural-musical phenomenon in the early development of what became commonly known as the hard bop / soul jazz subgenre of music. Art Blakey and Horace Silver together are often cited as the most prolific ambassadors of the hard bop evolution. Leonard Feather cites the invitation to trumpeter Blue Mitchell to join Silver's quintet as placing Mitchell "in the forefront of modern jazz" at the time; the same could be said of Cook.[11] Jazz producer and Mosaic Records cofounder Michael Cuscuna noted that the Horace Silver quintet was "incredibly popular" and placed the group in the same circle as Art Blakey's Jazz Messengers and the Clifford Brown–Max Roach group. Journalist Mike Davenport, in a review of *Doin' the Thing: The Horace Silver Quintet at the Village Gate* (Blue Note, 1961), declared Silver the "undisputed leader of the neo-bop school of jazz." Davenport noted that most people credit Art Blakey with that title, but he underscored that Silver was the musical director for Blakey's early groups and was "largely responsible" for the Blakey group's distinctive style.[12]

Within the Silver group, Cook was filling Mobley's front-man shoes ably. Biographer Piero Scaruffi cited Mobley's as "one of the most recognizable 'sounds' in hard bop, neither torrential like Coltrane's nor mellow like Stan Getz's."[13] In three years Mobley had already recorded himself into jazz history, with an array of Silver standards, including "The Preacher" (*Horace Silver and the Jazz Messengers*, Blue Note, 1955), "Señor Blues" (*Six Pieces of Silver*, Blue Note, 1956), "Cool Eyes" (which Silver referred to as his theme song) (*Six Pieces of Silver*), and "Home Cookin'" (*The Stylings of Silver*, Blue Note, 1957), among others. Mike Falcon, in an online review of Derek Ansell's "Workout: The Music of Hank Mobley," cited Mobley as the second most recorded artist on the Blue Note label, next to Jimmy Smith.[14] A 2018 article in the UK's *The Spectator* declared Mobley "the greatest sax player you never heard," and author Andrew L. Shea portrayed Mobley's tenor voice as "bluesy but not clichéd, soulful but smart, and with little of the caustic bark with which Rollins and Coltrane muscled out their improvisations."[15]

Cook was no clone of Mobley, but they were contemporaries on the New York jazz scene, and Cook acknowledged Mobley's influence on his playing. Cook succeeded Mobley in both the Dizzy Gillespie and Horace Silver bands. Was Cook "copying" Mobley if he played something similar to what Mobley had improvised at an earlier date? Not necessarily. It's plausible, Cook having acknowledged Mobley's influence, that Cook may have taken some styling cues and improvisational choices that followed Mobley's mold, or that Cook and Mobley both claim the same influences, were listening to the same saxophone masters, and that the improvisational milieu at that time favored certain approaches, licks, and patterns. Another hypothesis is that Mobley and Cook both could have been taking cues from the bandleader, Silver, and executing Silver's vision for his own group. Whatever the reason, there are some occasional similarities in the Mobley and Cook approaches. For example, the first measure of Cook's two-measure solo break on Horace Silver's "Nica's Dream" (recorded in 1960 as part of Silver's quintet) starts with a B-flat minor figure identical to a motif in the first measure of Mobley's own solo break on the same song four years earlier (recorded in 1956, as part of the Jazz Messengers, which included Silver on piano).

Hank Mobley's solo break, "Nica's Dream" (*The Jazz Messengers*, Columbia Records, 1956). The solo excerpt is transcribed for B-flat instruments.

Junior Cook's solo break, "Nica's Dream" (*Horace-Scope*, Blue Note, 1960. The solo excerpt is transcribed for B-flat instruments.

Silver's composition "Tippin'" also provides a canvas to compare and contrast Mobley's and Cook's improvisational approaches. Mobley recorded "Tippin'" for Silver's *Six Pieces of Silver* album, and Cook recorded "Tippin'" with Silver during the Newport Jazz Festival in 1958. Whether milieu or mimicry, in both solos we hear a fair portion of dominant bebop scale, eighth-note momentum, period jazz vocabulary, and some loitering on the major-seventh degree of the tonal center (the end of Mobley's second chorus of improvisation in 1956, and the end of Cook's first and second choruses in 1958) in this lesser-played rhythm changes tune.

Blue Mitchell recounted in an interview how Silver's group was a jazz classroom, helping him develop musically and honing his improvisational dexterity in the context of Silver's unique compositional style:

> The learning process was really intense. [Silver's] book was made up of originals and many of his tunes did not fall into the usual 8, 16, or 32-bar phrases. As soon as he realized I was having difficulty, he took me under his wing and had me drop by his house for some personal rehearsals. And I wasn't the only one he did that with either. We'd go over certain sections of tunes like "Out-law" or "No Smoking," and he'd play two or three bars that were giving me a hard time over and over 'til I had to ask him to stop. He was extremely intense.[16]

Contributing editor Barbara Gardner also described the discipline required of playing in the Silver band in a June 1963 cover feature of Horace Silver in *DownBeat* magazine. The feature included pictures of Silver and a picture of Cook and Mitchell but not of the other band members: "Rehearsals are not haphazard, run-through occurrences. The quintet members are expected to attend regularly, to arrive promptly, and to settle down to work immediately. Rehearsals are as exacting as a classroom theory hour. Each member, including Silver, is like a student-teacher; they all try experiments and instruct each other. But it does become the task of the leader to tie the lesson together for the benefit of the group."[17]

Author Ted Gioia contrasted the Blakey and Silver bands, asserting that while the Blakey band broke with its "rhythm-and-blues orientation" at the end of the "[Lee] Morgan–[Bobby] Timmons–[Benny] Golson unit," Silver maintained the path of funk/R&B-inflected music. Silver's compositions also brought a diversity by exploring non-4/4 rhythms and Silver's Portuguese cultural roots, all within the framework of his musical vision. Gioia summarized Silver's vision thus: "His [Silver's] sound is uncluttered. His melodies are succinct and memorable. The rhythms are propulsive without being overbearing. The obsession with virtuosity, so characteristic of bebop, is almost entirely absent and never missed."[18]

Cook also walked into what may have been one of the last true sweet spots where the Venn diagram of jazz and popular music overlapped. Many of Silver's compositions, released as singles, were popular jukebox hits. Cuscuna noted the importance of compositions to the popularity of Silver's quintet and of other groups as well: "In those days, it was all about the tunes."[19] The Jazztet, for example, had the benefit of Benny Golson's compositional skill. While Art Blakey was not a prolific composer, he hired musicians like Golson and Wayne Shorter, who contributed a wealth of great material. Those compositions secured work for the groups. Swinging, catchy tunes secured airplay on jazz radio stations across the country, and airplay brought popular buzz and recognition that spawned gigs around the country for the musicians. Ted Gioia writes that many critics "dismissed this 'soul jazz' style out of hand" but "listeners responded with enthusiasm" and the subgenre generated "airplay, jukebox spins, and brisk record sales."[20] Silver's popularity was buoyed by Blue Note support; *DownBeat* magazines featured full-page advertisements declaring "Horace Silver Pianist—Composer—Arranger—Leader . . . Extraordinaire," pushing Silver's latest album, and reminding readers of his previous releases as well. One such ad promoted Silver's *Blowin' the Blues Away* album in December 1959; another full-page ad in the June 1963 *DownBeat* (the issue with the cover feature of Silver) spotlighted several album covers of "The Original—The Inventive—The Exciting" Horace

Silver, from *Horace Silver and the Jazz Messengers* to his latest album at the time, *The Tokyo Blues*.[21]

Hard bop was an evolution in jazz from the bebop school of up tempos and complex harmonies and chord changes. No one danced to bebop; in fact, some New York City clubs famously posted "No dancing" signs in their quarters. Bebop, in that regard, was deliberately sanctified and set apart. The architects of bebop music set the tempos and the changes to distance themselves from what they likely viewed as the more placid, background music vibe of the swing-era bands.

Hard bop, however, conjured descriptions as earthy, bluesy, down home, soulful, and, perhaps most tellingly for broad popular appeal, "accessible." Author Andrew Shea described hard bop concisely as "a response to both the cushy pleasantness of West Coast jazz and the introverted intellectualism of New York bebop. The name [Jazz] 'Messengers,' with its evangelical overtones, hints at the inflections of gospel and blues that would give hard bop its audience-friendly flavour. No more beatnik berets and professorial pipes—with hard bop, swing was most definitely the thing."[22]

Whereas in bebop the soloist and the individual improvised solos were the focus of attention, in hard bop one found a direct thread back to a hallmark of the swing bands of old: arrangement. Hard bop also featured improvised solos, but interspersed in the music were arranged interludes, channels, and shout choruses. Producer Michael Cuscuna, for example, described one of Silver's compositions, "The Outlaw," in the liner notes for the album *Horace Silver: Live at Newport '58*: "a 13-bar line, the last six of which are over a Latin rhythm, played twice, then a 10-bar bridge, a 16-bar Latin vamp, and a two-bar tag."[23] Often these interludes were not improvised. They were crafted in advance to maintain a song's energy and help the audience along to, as Silver put it, help the band "find a groove." Arrangements and interludes were frequent in Silver's compositions and were leveraged more broadly across groups of the time; think of the trademark drum solo at the top of the Jazz Messengers' treatment of Benny Golson's "Blues March" and the stock interlude of Golson's "Whisper Not"; the piano call and horn response of Bobby Timmons's "Moanin'"; the interlude of Timmons's "Dat Dere"; the Clifford Brown–Max Roach quintet's intro mimicking of a "Parisian Thoroughfare" soundscape; the driving, perfect-fifth eighth notes in the stereotyped "Indian" drone that Brown, Roach, and tenorist Harold Land use to open their rendition of "Cherokee"; or the rhythmically rich through-composition of Brown, Roach, and Land's treatment of "I Get a Kick Out of You."

It should be noted here, both for reference and for further study, how "urban" and "folk" occupied the same space in the development of jazz genres. Some sources, including Kenny Mathieson's *Cookin': Hard Bop and Soul Jazz 1954–65*, infer a paradoxical relationship between the two: "[Hard bop] was also a music with a distinctly urban ambiance, despite all those throwbacks to rural forms," like "the blues, rhythm and blues, and even folk forms."[24] This, however, is a false dichotomy, neglecting the prominent influence of the Great Migration of African Americans from Southern locales to Northern states for employment opportunities and a better, or just different, life. Junior Cook himself set up shop in New York City after being raised in Pensacola, Florida, part of McGovern's so-called new South and an apparent middle ground between old South Alabama and Mississippi and the heavily urban South Florida locales like Miami or Orlando. New York City–based Dizzy Gillespie was born and raised in Cheraw, South Carolina. John Coltrane, born in 1926, migrated to Philadelphia in the mid-1940s from High Point, North Carolina. Decoupling the "urban" and the "folk" or "rural" in this context is a fool's errand: many of the standard-bearers of bebop and hard bop, if not born and raised in the rural South, likely were surrounded by those same influences in the Northern urban cities by the migration of African Americans, who brought their musical forms and influences with them. As Southern Blacks migrated north, their traditions and forms were concentrated within the Black community based on segregationist housing and employment norms at the time. So, too, did the likes of Coltrane, Cook, and many others cut their teeth as apprentices in their musical careers by playing in rhythm and blues bands, in some cases traveling the Southern Chitlin' Circuit in their early careers. Coltrane played with the Earl Bostic band. Bill Hardman, with whom Cook would team up in a fiery, adventurous quintet in the 1980s, toured with rhythm and blues bandleader Tiny Bradshaw in the 1950s. Cook, for his part, joined the likes of rhythm and blues singer Willie Mabon and the Dell Tones early in his career.

The Blue Mitchell–Junior Cook partnership continued the trumpet–tenor saxophone front line that marked most iterations of Horace Silver's bands. Summing it up, Duck Baker noted it simply odd that "the lineup of trumpeter Blue Mitchell, tenor saxophonist Junior Cook, bassist Gene Taylor, and drummer Roy Brooks isn't often named among the great ensembles of the era," continuing that "few bands could beat this one for swing, good humor, excellent soloing and, above all, group chemistry."[25] Silver did not invent the trumpet–tenor saxophone front line, but he executed that ensemble grouping very efficiently to make his melodies—often written with tight harmonies—come alive. Silver himself called Mitchell and Cook "an incredible pair," according to the liner notes for Cook's *Good Cookin'* album; Herb Wong, who authored those notes, cited Mitchell and Cook as forming a "consistently tight, sympatico twosome of horns." Bill Shoemaker, in a Horace Silver retrospective, also underscored the Blue Mitchell–Junior Cook edition, more than any other personnel aggregation of the Silver quintet, as conveying superlative "ensemble cohesion and interpretive spark."[26]

Silver's melodies often incorporated tight harmonies, including close intervals. For example, the successive major-second harmonies in measure 10 of "Kiss Me Right" resonate with Mitchell and Cook playing the same octave on their respective horns. In Silver's "Tokyo Blues," measure 13 features a crunchy major-second interval to highlight the progression to the F7 chord.

Cook quickly gained his footing in the Silver group, likely from the "intense learning process" that Mitchell described. Cook had a few very early stumbles: one can hear on the *Live at Newport '58* album (released in 2008) that Cook seemed to miss forms; on "Cool Eyes," for example, he missed the tag that separated solos. He also seemed a little less surefooted within solos, starting lines and cutting them off abruptly. On later albums, however, starting with *Finger Poppin'*, Cook demonstrated a "deliberateness" in his improvisation, an approach that reviews would describe as "solid," "thoughtful," and "constructive."[27] Trumpeter Valery Ponomarev summarized Cook's improvisations as marked by "precision," perhaps as clear a nod as any to the influence of Sonny Stitt on Cook's tenor playing.[28] Stitt for his part is known not for cliché, but for a comprehensive mastery of bebop vocabulary and a delivery that in some cases harks to classical music in its accuracy. Perhaps of his own accord and perhaps a result of Silver's own vision for the group, Cook does not let his solos go to abandon. His delivery is surefooted and exact, a trait that would follow him for most of his career, even to his very last recordings on the SteepleChase label.

Like Mobley under Silver's headship, Cook waxed himself into jazz history by contributing his sound and solos to several of Silver's best-known compositions. From the album *Finger Poppin'* (Blue Note, January 1959), Silver's hits included "Cookin' at the Continental," "Come On Home," and "Juicy Lucy." "Cookin' at the Continental" is a rollicking, jump blues–type tune complete with trumpet–tenor sax melodic call (measures 1–7) and a piano response (measure 8) and a four-measure break within the melody that propels the tune toward solos. "Come On Home" is a loping, pimp-walking minor blues, the melody patiently rationed out in six- and eight-syllable increments. Jazz vocal legend Jon Hendricks matched vocalese lyrics to Cook's solo in "Come On Home" on Lambert, Hendricks, and Ross's cover of the song on their self-titled album on the Columbia label (1961), further immortalizing Cook's solo. "Juicy Lucy," by contrast, ups the tempo to a brisk walk, a contrafact of Charlie Parker's "Confirmation" in a "Bird blues" form, a variation on the basic blues form with a bridge added.

A *DownBeat* magazine review in July 1959 declared Silver's *Finger Poppin'* album "hard-swinging jazz from New York, blessed by good soloists" and gave the album four stars. The four-star review guaranteed that the album would get subsequent press in the magazine; *DownBeat* also featured a "Jazz Record Buyer's Guide" section, which listed "jazz LPs rated four stars or more during the previous five-issue period."[29] The *DownBeat* review inaccurately claimed that the album "appears to be tenor man Cook's debut on record," but nonetheless reported that Cook "shows himself to be an intense, thoughtful, and constructive soloist, not in a hurry to say his piece and making his contributions mean something." The review concluded that Cook "[flexed] his muscles" on "Mellow D," the last tune on the album.[30]

From the album *Blowin' the Blues Away* (Blue Note, 1959), Cook was featured on "Blowin' the Blues Away," "Sister Sadie," and "Peace" (Mitchell and Cook play the melody line on "Peace" but only Silver solos on the tune). The title track is a street race of a tune, hurtling with abandon with the bands' collective foot on the musical gas from start to finish. After tenor, trumpet, and piano solos, Cook and Mitchell exchange the lead down the stretch, trading "twos" (two measures each) until they launch in unison into a shout chorus before returning to the melody, also known in jazz parlance as the "head." Cook describes "Sister Sadie" (and another Silver hit, "Filthy McNasty") as "monsters" he created, possibly alluding to his contribution to those tunes' popularity. "Sister Sadie" is close to a textbook version of the hard bop formula of the time: 1) an uncomplicated, hummable melody 2) that repeats with minor variation 3) call and response between the melody-carrying horns and Silver's maintenance of the primary tonality;[31] 4) a swinging, driving B section that introduces a second motif; 5) "backgrounds"—Blue Mitchell's "shoutin' John" trumpet bursts underneath the second chorus of Cook's solo to spur him on—and 6) an arranged, let-it-all-out shout chorus that takes the band back to the head.

"Blowin the Blues Away" earned five stars, the highest rating, in a review penned by Ralph J. Gleason in *DownBeat*'s 21 January 1960 issue. Gleason wrote the LP was a "lovely album," full of "fire and brimstone" and "revivalistic carrying on," pandering to the gospel influences commonly associated with hard bop and soul jazz. Gleason called Cook a "good, solidly blowing tenor" and noted that the group as a whole had an "*esprit de combo* here which is great to find," summarizing that "we're going to be playing this [album] for a long time."[32]

On *Horace-Scope* (Blue Note, 1960), the Silver classics-to-be include "Strollin'" and "Nica's Dream" (which Kenny Burrell first recorded for his Blue Note album *K. B. Blues* [Blue Note, 1957]).

Silver debuted his composition "Filthy McNasty" on the album *Doin' the Thing* (Blue Note, 1961), a live recording at New York City's Village Gate club. Cook also took tenor saxophone credit on Silver's "The Tokyo Blues" on an album of the same name (Blue Note, 1962), which earned a four-star rating in a record review in *DownBeat*'s 22 November 1962 issue. The review declared the Silver quintet "the most consistently rewarding purveyor of the hard-burning, blues-drenched version of modern jazz (usually labelled 'funk' or 'soul jazz')" and attributed the consistency both to Silver's "strong musical direction and the fact that like players have succeeded each other in the band."[33]

Cook acknowledged in the 1959 interview his love of ballads and appeared almost to lament that Silver's quintet had few ballads in the repertoire but, rather, "focus[ed] on funk."[34] He craved to give ballads "a blues twist" in the context of the Silver Quintet. Some seventeen years later, Cook, perhaps making up for lost time, takes frontline control as the sole horn on the ballads "When Sunny Gets Blue" and the Monk composition "Pannonica" during a live performance in Germany with the Louis Hayes–Junior Cook Quintet (*Louis Hayes/Junior Cook Quintet: At Onkel Po's Carnegie Hall, Hamburg 1976*, Jazzline Records [2019]).

(Now, "funk" is one of those words with a chameleon quality and should be considered in the proper temporal context associated with Silver and the late 1950s. Buddy Bolden's "Funky Butt" funk, among the early uses of the blues on brass instruments to expand the ragtime genre, was not the same as Horace Silver's funk. Horace Silver's funk paradoxically could be considered "secular church"—bringing blues and gospel influences, shout choruses, hearty stops and starts, and interludes into the jazz form. And the Bolden, Silver, and Blakey funk are light years from the Maceo Parker, Mandrills, and Funkadelic funk some twenty years later. Funk of this latter era was a musical potion of an amplified rhythm and blues form with electric instruments and a healthy portion of Black power.)

The steady dose of advertising and media attention contributed to keeping the Silver quintet in the eye and the ear of the jazz industry. *DownBeat*'s 20 June 1963 issue featured Silver on the cover, along with a cover story entitled "Inside the Horace Silver Quintet."[35] In the piece Silver extolled the unity between Cook and Mitchell: "Junior and Blue work so tight . . . they sometimes sound like one instrument." The article also underscored the esprit de corps within the group; the author asserted that "each musician is considered an excellent technician and driving expressionist in his own right—yet the group has no star," and the piece quoted Silver himself declaring, "This is the best band I've ever had." The issue also featured a lead sheet—"A New Silver composition-arrangement"—of Silver's composition "Silver's Serenade," a bonus prize for the reader like some cereal-box toy (pages 40–41).

Cook's output, and Silver's apparent satisfaction with it, led to a six-year tenure with the Silver Quintet. Art Blakey, by contrast, was famous for keeping his musicians in circulation. Sometimes Blakey was ready for newer, younger sounds; on other occasions Blakey effectively sent musicians on their way, feeling that they were ready to take their careers to the next level by leading their own bands. Silver seemed more content to keep a good thing going.[36]

Cook and Mitchell's association with the Horace Silver quintet from 1958 through 1964 was the longest of any saxophone-trumpet front line in that ensemble. The last complete recording with the Silver band was *Silver's Serenade* on Blue Note, released in 1963. The album included "Silver's Serenade," "Let's Get to the Nitty Gritty" (Silver used the same title for his autobiography years later), "Sweet Sweetie Dee," "The Dragon Lady," and "Nineteen Bars." "The Dragon Lady," with its gonglike cymbal crashes and quartal (built with pitches an interval of a fourth apart) harmonies evoke an Eastern sensibility. (One wonders if "The Dragon Lady" was a leftover composition that didn't make Silver's previous album, *The Tokyo Blues*.) Cook's improvisation on "The Dragon Lady" in particular—faster runs, range of the horn scalar leaps—sound Coltrane-ish, possibly a glimpse of an improvisational arc to come and, in its urgency, almost introduces the saxophone sound of Joe Henderson, who would succeed Cook in the Silver band within a year.

Silver's decision to break up that group and introduce new personnel came at the suggestion of Blue Note producer Alfred Lion. According to Cuscuna, Silver had recorded three tunes in 1964 and didn't like the recorded outputs.[37] Silver, very particular and detail oriented, knew exactly what he wanted, and cuts that may sound fine to the listener's ear may have been lacking some intangible spark that indicated a finished product in Silver's ear. At Lion's suggestion Silver set things in motion to switch out band members and find new personnel for his quintet.

Cook's time in the Silver quintet—certainly for so long a tenure—not only provided a wealth of experience but also did much to establish him within music circles, even if not in critics' polls or in making him a household name among the jazz public. Cook remembered his time with Silver, and his stint before that with Gillespie, as "unbelievable" and a "dream come true," touting that his first trip to Europe was with Silver's band.[38] The opportunity for musicians to play in these seminal bands was like "their degree, their credentials," according to Cuscuna: "'Oh, he's working with Horace!' They could ride their life on it, and deservedly so, because you couldn't be a slouch and work" with musicians like Silver and Art Blakey.[39] Tenor saxophonist Javon Jackson also spoke of the sense of membership from being an alum of those iconic bands. For example, Jackson's own tenure in the Jazz Messengers connected him with fellow Jazz Messengers alum Freddie Hubbard and opened an opportunity for him to join Hubbard's group.[40]

Joe and Junior, Junior and Joe

Comparisons between Cook and saxophonist Joe Henderson—in interviews for this work and in history—bubbled up early and often. Some of Cook's friends and musical associates perceived that Cook's contribution to jazz had been overlooked in favor of Henderson and were eager to set the record straight—or at least provide more balance on the topic.

It is no slight—to Cook or to Henderson—to claim that they, as musical contemporaries, share a musical concept to some degree, just as two individuals can share a Texas drawl or a Boston accent yet still have distinct and individual voices. The drawl *belongs* to neither individual; it is a manifestation of their common environment. Both individuals, coming from that environment, display that trait; they share the drawl and may express certain common words, slang, or idiomatic expressions (like *y'all*). They share a dialect and yet each have their own voice. Acknowledging Cook's and Henderson's proximity as contemporaries does not deny them each their singular voice in the jazz idiom.

Cook and Henderson roomed together for an unspecified period of time after Henderson's release from the US Army and arrival in New York

City in 1962, according to several secondary sources. An interview with Henderson affirms some level of association between the two tenormen. Henderson said:

> Trane [John Coltrane] formed his own group and Miles called me to take Trane's place. Uncle Sam called at the same time. Uncle Sam with all of that fire-power won over Miles. I knew John very well. As a matter of fact, I knew the chick he married, Alice McLeod. She was from Detroit. I knew her for a long time before I met John. She would talk about John all the time. I would ask, "Who is this John cat, I play the tenor." She would talk about John like he was a god. I went out of town one time for about six weeks, and when I got back Junior Cook said, "Joe, guess what? John has got your old lady." She wanted to really get off into something heavy. I just didn't have eyes for that at that time. I was just getting to New York and trying to find my way around.[41]

Bobby Watson acknowledged the sympatico between Junior and Joe in a *Jazz Times* article in 2019 and also noted that Henderson ultimately achieved more notoriety: "Junior was one of those cats who would hang in the shadows [at a club], and then once he heard some good music he would appear out of nowhere. On recordings, he and Joe Henderson have a lot in common—I wonder who got what from whom. Junior Cook was Horace Silver's tenor player before Joe Henderson was, and when I first heard "Chick's Tune" [with Cook on tenor saxophone, from Blue Mitchell's album *The Thing to Do*] I thought it was Joe. But Joe gets his acknowledgment and Junior is still under the radar."[42]

Michael Cuscuna and Horace Silver both noticed the similarity as well, in a story that Cuscuna retold:

> We [Cuscuna and Horace Silver] were listening to some tapes of Horace's band, live with Joe, you know, and I said, sometimes it sounds . . . some of his [Henderson's] lines, especially on that . . . the bottom octave of the sax, it reminds me of Junior Cook. And Horace said, "Yeah, me too." You know? [Horace continued.] "And I said that to Joe once, and he was offended by that." I guess Joe wanted to be

> considered to be totally original. But that [Joe's reaction to Silver's comment] kinda surprised me because I think some of Joe . . . maybe it's because of Horace's compositions but I always thought that some of Joe at that point came out of Junior . . . and some of Horace. Maybe we were wrong.[43]

A Freddie Hubbard interview also amplified the connection between Cook and Henderson: "Well, Joe (Henderson) . . . Joe came to Brooklyn back in the '60s and he moved in with Junior Cook. I had been playing around Brooklyn with Junior Cook before he joined Horace Silvers [*sic*]. And they both (Joe and Junior) sound alike for a long time. You couldn't tell the difference between . . . a lot between Joe Henderson and Junior Cook, and they both ended up working with Horace Silvers. And I think Joe stretched out a little more, you know, got a bigger name and did a lot of records with different people."[44]

The same anecdotes seemed to circulate among musicians regarding the relationship between Cook and Henderson. Musicians recounted that Cook "went out of his way" to help Henderson get established in New York. Several biographical sketches highlight that Henderson met trumpeter Kenny Dorham during a party at Cook's apartment, leading to an association that helped lift off Henderson's career. Vocalist Timmy Shepherd remembered that Cook displayed a palpable sense of hurt when Shepherd had mentioned Henderson's name; Cook retold a story to Shepherd of hearing rumors that Henderson was bad-mouthing Cook to other musicians. Cook also told Shepherd that he arrived at one of Henderson's club dates and, after Cook approached him, Henderson had brushed him off and acted as if he didn't know him. Shepherd said that he never mentioned Henderson to Cook again.[45]

Contemporaries of Cook and Henderson cast doubt on Henderson's claim to have given lessons to Cook. Henderson asserted as much in an interview with George Shaw circa 1979. Henderson's comments were in response to a question about teaching improvisation to "students": "A lot of cats studied with me when I lived in Detroit. Junior Cook and Pat La Barbera are some of the cats who have studied with me. Junior played with

Freddie [Hubbard] for awhile. Pat is with Elvin [Jones]. That helps me to believe that it is working."[46]

Contemporaries find it more likely that Henderson and Cook "shedded" together—practicing, trading ideas and inspiration, and learning from one another—rather than had any explicit teacher-student relationship as implied in that one excerpt of Henderson's interview. Others perceived Cook and Henderson as having a similar concept of sound but pegged Cook's approach as more relaxed, singing and flowing. Trombonist Curtis Fuller, who roomed with Henderson at Wayne State University, reportedly affirmed, based apparently on his own observation of Henderson's development over time, that Henderson "got a lot" from Cook.[47] Modern tenorman Bill Pierce, an alum of Art Blakey's Jazz Messengers, acknowledged the similar sound concept: "But this was his [Cook's] sound: he was really relaxed, could really swing, and had a really melodic sort of way of playing. I always thought of Joe Henderson as like . . . Junior Cook on acid or something because it was a little bit more energetic in a sense . . . in a sense." Richard Cook, in *Blue Note Records: The Biography*, similarly described that Henderson's tenure with the Horace Silver quintet seemed to tame Henderson's approach, which, outside Silver's group, was "a good deal more turbulent and anxious."[48] Even within Silver's group on occasion, Henderson tended toward the more "turbulent": consider Henderson's wailing, false-finger screams on Silver's "African Queen" from the *Cape Verdean Blues* album (Blue Note, 1966) or the mosquito-buzzing first seven bars of his solo on "Que Pasa?" from the *Song for My Father* album (Blue Note, 1964), both of which are in stark contrast to Cook's more consistently Mobley-esque approach to the tenor. Silver's "Tokyo Blues" also documents Cook's Jekyll to Henderson's Hyde (of the time): Cook's two recorded bites at the "Tokyo Blues" apple (Silver's *Tokyo Blues* album [Blue Note, 1962] and a later recording of the same tune in Paris, also in 1962) both present patient, flowing melodicism. A recording with Silver's band at Antibes (1964), by stark contrast, shows Henderson reaching seemingly for Cook's antithesis: everything *but* flowing eighth notes and harmonies boldly at odds with the Silver's foundation in a performance that exposes the understatement in Barry McRae's *Jazz Journal* description of Joe Henderson as bringing "to the group a slightly more modern approach" when he replaced Cook in Silver's quintet.[49] A review of Cook's *On a Misty Night* release in 1991 also brought to the fore the interplay between Cook and Henderson: "If Cook's role in forming the conception of Silver's quintet is overlooked, so is his influence as a saxophonist, particularly on the man who replaced him in Silver's band: Joe Henderson. Cook's dark, reedy sound and his skittering rhythms were refined and extended by Henderson. Ironically, it seems as if Cook was then later influenced by Henderson himself. Cook's '70s recordings with the Louis Hayes and Woody Shaw quintet, which exhibit an even greater harmonic scope and rhythmic looseness than before, are especially evocative of Henderson."[50]

Cook and Henderson certainly ran in some of the same musical circles, crisscrossing one another in the bands of the day. Henderson, for example, succeeded Cook in the Horace Silver quintet when Silver changed personnel in 1964, contributing to Silver's arguably most famous hit, "Song for My Father," on an album that featured tracks from two recording sessions, some with Henderson and other early recorded tracks with Cook. Later, Cook trailed Henderson: Henderson was part of the short-lived Jazz Communicators (1967–1968), which featured trumpet player Freddie Hubbard and drummer Louis Hayes.[51] Cook would have his own turn in those lineups after Henderson, rounding out Freddie Hubbard's quintet for recording sessions and live performances in the early 1970s and later teaming up with Hayes in the Louis Hayes–Junior Cook Quintet that featured trumpet sensation Woody Shaw in the later 1970s. It's an odd coincidence that the March 1992 issue of *DownBeat* magazine, the first issue after Cook's death in February 1992, had featured Joe Henderson on the cover. The two saxophone stalwarts crisscrossed one last time.

Chapter 3

In Demand (Later Years)

I knew Junior when he was at Berklee. He and I played in an ensemble.
Of course I was extremely intimidated by his presence.
—Bill Pierce

In Demand (Later Years)

Cook found himself marked—branded, almost—by the impact of his six years with the Silver band as a character actor pigeonholed into a particular movie role: villain's muscular henchman; petty robber; effete hair stylist; brooding, cynical detective; hard bop saxophone-playing sideman. Character actors are working actors, however. They find work if they bring the role to life and if their character is in demand. Cook's character was definitely in demand during the next twenty years of his life—which also turned out to be the last twenty years of his life—as he received consistent calls to play as a sideman in the bands of jazz heavy hitters.

Cook recorded comparatively few sessions as leader. The Jazzland label released Cook's first recording as leader, *Junior's Cookin'*, in 1962. *DownBeat's* Harvey Pekar had faint praise for *Junior's Cookin'*, giving it a two-and-a-half star rating, assessing that Cook channeled more Lester Young in his "not large" tone and "restrained" playing even at rapid tempos: "Because [Cook] is disinclined to attempt to play any ideas that are not ordinary, his solos, though never bad, are rarely memorable. On most tracks in this album he seems content to make the changes. This he does but little more. Only on 'Easy Living' does he communicate much emotion."[1] Pekar concludes that Blue Mitchell's trumpet playing, though "not quite at the top of his form here," is "easily the most interesting feature of the album."[2] Another review of *Junior's Cookin'* cast Cook as "mainstream modern," falling generally "into the Sonny Stitt–Hank Mobley bag." Cook is the "newest of these" mainstream modern players, the review declared: "His phrasing is spare, he has a strong tone, and he swings like mad."[3]

A review of *Junior's Cookin'* on the website *AllAboutJazz* contends that Cook's album was a recording of convenience. The Riverside record label was making a series of albums with Blue Mitchell as leader, and since Cook was present to support Mitchell's recordings, the Riverside label took the opportunity to produce an album with Cook as leader as well, released on its Jazzland subsidiary label, which was established in 1960.[4]

Cook's next leader dates were relatively few and far between, shoehorned into his steady career as a sideman until the series of SteepleChase releases in the last five years of his life. Though Cook organized a relatively steady regimen of live performances in which he led the show (i.e., the Junior Cook Quartet,) proportionally Cook appears to have spent more time as sideman than as leader during his musical career.

(Pianist Michael Weiss, however, presented an alternate viewpoint, surmising that some players are effectively forced into leader roles and finding their own gigs because they are not getting enough calls and work as sidemen to sustain themselves. Cook's apparent lack of focus on developing himself on the scene as a leader could simply have been testament to his success, and consistent calls, as a sideman.[5])

It is clear from Cook's discography that he preferred playing extant repertoire rather than composing his own tunes. Cook's *Junior's Cookin'* would have been a prime canvas to showcase both his playing and compositional skills. Yet the album instead featured the compositions of Roland Alexander ("Myzar" and "Pleasure Bent"), pianist Dolo Coker ("Field Day"), Charles Davis ("Turbo Village"), Blue Mitchell ("Blue Farouq" and "Sweet Cakes"), and a Leo Robin–Ralph Rainger jazz standard ("Easy Living"). Bill Hardman encouraged Cook to compose, soliciting tunes from him to feature in the Hardman–Cook quintet's sets in the 1980s, but Cook apparently did not deliver. Cook countered that he was "always composing [i.e., improvising] when I'm on the bandstand," according to Shepherd.[6] It's unknown whether that counter was an authentic reflection of Cook's philosophy of some higher-order improvision-as-composition, a cop-out to avoid answering the question, or both.

The one observed composition credited to Cook, a tune entitled "Junior's Cook," was recorded on Cook's 1992 SteepleChase release, *You Leave Me Breathless*, one of his last recordings before his death. Russia-born trumpeter Valery Ponomarev, who played trumpet on *You Leave Me Breathless*, however, noted that the tune entitled "Junior's Cook" and credited to Cook actually was his composition. The same tune was recorded on Ponomarev's album *Live at Vartan Jazz* (Vartan Jazz label, 1995) under the name "One for Morgans." (Ponomarev concluded the composition credit to Cook as a simple error or misrepresentation by the publishers.)[7] Vocalist Timmy Shepherd recalled that Cook had composed a tune called "Beatrice," named after Cook's companion in the 1980s. Shepherd heard Cook play the tune on piano but not in any public performances.

Cook's penchant for recording others' compositions also affected his bottom line and may reflect a lack of business acumen, marketing skill, or ability to fully commodify his talents. The general parameters of a recording contract of the day might include an artist fee and artist royalties, if the album sold sufficient quantities to cover the costs involved in the recording. Pianist Mickey Tucker recalls that the union fee of the day may have been in the area of $500. With no compositions from Cook's own pen on his recordings, Cook denied himself royalties from copyright and publishing. Tucker surmises that he himself probably made more money from Cook's recordings than Cook, in that Tucker received publishing and writer royalties from the Tucker compositions that Cook recorded.

In aggregate Cook's recording career seems prodigious for the time. Outside of a handful of gaps, Cook recorded and was featured on at least one recording release per year from 1958 until 1991: 1958–1968, 1971–1974, 1977, 1979, 1981, 1984, and 1988–1991. Some of the recording gaps corresponded to Cook's touring around the world with some of jazz's best bands (discussed further in the next chapter)—for example, with Freddie Hubbard in the late 1960s and early 1970s and with Louis Hayes in the mid-1970s—and in some cases recordings were made of those very bands in those time periods, but the music was released decades later. While Cook's recordings as leader kept his face and tenor sound in the eyes and ears of jazz listeners, each recording endeavor (as leader or sideman) probably netted him only a one-time payout for services rendered.

The critics' view of Cook's playing was a mix of praise and dismissal. At least some of the dismissive attitude was likely born of the fact that some critics loved to hate the hard bop sound, reflected in reviews that hardly assessed any redeeming quality in hard bop releases. Maitland Edey's review of Silver's *Blowin' the Blues Away* in *Jazz Review* declared that Cook's playing was "unimpressive": "a brutish tone which permits no expressive shading, employs the narrowest possible range of dynamics, and suffers from lack of melodic imagination and stiff time." Edey concluded by imploring Cook to "crawl out of that tangle of repetitious hard-bop clichés."[8] A review of Dave Bailey's *One Foot in the Gutter* (Epic, 1960), featuring Cook as a sideman, received two stars from reviewer John S. Wilson, oozing with negativity:

> "Sandu" takes up all of the second side of the disc, and although, as might be expected, it fails to justify its length, it produces most of what little interesting playing developed at the session—a long, rocking lusty solo by Fuller and a flugelhorn opus by Terry that builds over an automobile horn riff by Fuller and Cook. But monotony takes over when Cook arrives at his solo, and Parlan lifts the soggy blanket only slightly before battering the piece down to a new depth of tedium with his favorite banality. . . . The recording was made before a small, friendly audience. Routine announcements by Bailey have been faithfully preserved, including, of all idiocies, introductions of, and applause for, each of the musicians.[9]

On the other side, Carl Brauer's review of Cook's *Good Cookin'* (Muse, 1979) in *Cadence* magazine declared the album "manna from heaven for starving hard bop fans," "hard-driving, swinging hard bop in the tradition of Blue Note's halcyon days."[10]

Blue Mitchell

Following the Silver band, Cook and Blue Mitchell continued the Silver vibe in a Silver quintet sans Silver. In fact, Mitchell and Cook began to blossom their own thing even while still in Silver's band. Cook's first recording as leader, *Junior's Cookin'*, on the Jazzland label, was released in 1962 with Mitchell on trumpet. That same year Mitchell released *The Cup Bearers* on the Riverside label, with Cook on tenor. Mitchell continued to release albums via Blue Note Records in subsequent years, also with Cook: *The Thing to Do* (1964), *Down with It* (1965), and *Bring It Home to Me* and *Boss Horn* (1966). A *Melody Maker* review of Mitchell's *Down with It* album pegged Cook as "a forceful player" who "may not figure high up in the polls" but "always turns in a highly-listenable performance."[11] Cook reportedly spent an unspecified period of time living in California in a cottage in the back of the Mitchells' family home.[12]

Cook's performances on Mitchell's albums continued the Silver legacy: the forms, discipline (some may say "reserve"), and blues and gospel infusion that marked Silver's foundational contributions to what are now described as the hard bop and soul jazz genres. The title track of Mitchell's *Bring It Home to Me* presents a slightly altered blues form. Cook's solo sounds almost entirely composed of notes from the blues scale (the minor pentatonic scale, adding the flatted fifth degree of the scale). "Bring It Home to Me" sounds like one of many attempts among jazz musicians and record labels to catch the lightning popularity of Lee Morgan's 1964 release, *The Sidewinder*, in a bottle for themselves. Other seeming attempts at replicating that rhythmic, driving boogaloo shuffle included Duke Pearson's "Millie" (recorded by Blue Mitchell in 1966); Wayne Shorter's "Adam's Apple" (1966); Stanley Turrentine's "And Satisfy" (1966), and Joe Henderson's "Mamacita" (1968).

Mitchell and Cook eventually split, possibly because Cook's laid-back style did not make for a good business partner. Mitchell reportedly grew frustrated with Cook because the latter didn't appear to have the energy or incentive to create product—be it more frequent recording sessions or penning his own compositions. Mitchell's wife, Thelma, ever watching out for her husband and his career and seldom one to mince words, suggested that Blue needed to find another musical collaborator, perceiving Cook as lazy.[13] Mitchell had recorded his first album as leader, *Big 6*, on the Riverside label in 1958; Horace Silver, introducing his band at their first concert in Paris on 14 February 1959, referred to his trumpeter as "Riverside recording artist Blue Mitchell."[14] Mitchell's *Big 6* was followed by *Blue Soul* in 1959 and *Smooth as the Wind* (with orchestra and strings, arranged and conducted by Tadd Dameron and Benny Golson) in 1960, all before the release of Cook's first recording as leader, *Junior's Cookin'*, in 1962.

Thelma Mitchell's caution to her husband likely was not aimed at Cook's musicianship, as Cook and Mitchell by that time had proven themselves quite a potent frontline duo both under Silver's leadership and beyond. Rather, Mitchell's wife may have been reacting to the perceived lack of business acumen and assertiveness that seemed to surround Cook and have greater and lesser effects on his career over time. Years later, likely alluding to the same, Woody Shaw III, referring to the personnel of the Louis Hayes–Junior Cook quintet featuring his father, Woody Shaw II, on trumpet, described Cook as "void of all pretenses or of the slightest indication of extra-musical 'ambition.'"[15] Whether lacking in financial knowledge, deficient in the business side of the music business, exhibiting a low sense of urgency for composition or recording as a leader, or born of the "super sensitive" self-doubt that made him try to tip out of the Dizzy Gillespie band rehearsal, Cook at once maintained a career as a jobbing musician and yet appeared to let opportunities slip past him.

* * * * * *

Cook lived in Brooklyn for a time in the 1960s, near Herkimer Street and New York Avenue, according to fellow saxophonist and friend Fred Daniels. Leonard Feather's *Encyclopedia of Jazz of the Sixties* listed Cook's address as 1331 Pacific Street, Brooklyn 16, NY.[16] Daniels recalled Cook as a regular at a Brooklyn jam session. The jam session location, which doubled as a boardinghouse of some sort, was called Sue's Pad, on McDougal Street. Walking into the basement jam session, Daniels remembers musicians representing a "who's who of album covers": Cedar Walton, Booker Ervin, Clifford Jordan, and Cook.

Cook relocated to the Boston area circa the late 1960s. Liner notes from Don Patterson's album *Opus de Don* (Prestige, 1968) noted that Cook traveled from Boston to play the recording session at Town Sound studios in Englewood, New Jersey. In the late 1960s and early 1970s, Cook lived in the Beacon Hill area of Boston, some two miles from the campus of Berklee College of Music.[17] He shared in an interview with broadcaster Leigh Kamman that he had visited Boston a few times with Silver's quintet and, following the stints with Silver and with Blue Mitchell, he had relocated to the city because he "met a young lady up there."[18]

The young lady that Cook met was Patricia Landry. The two met when Landry traveled to New York's East Side to visit a friend who had recently relocated there from Boston. The friend introduced Landry to Cook and they "hit it off immediately," Landry shared. They lived together in Boston for about ten years. Landry described Cook's devotion to his horn and to the music, recalling how he would play "every day, walking from room to room." Cook kept his horn beside the bed at night; Landry joked with him that he would probably sleep with the horn in the bed if he could do so comfortably. She summed up her assessment of Cook this way: "Music was his life."[19]

Cook taught at Berklee during this period, an "unexpected" opportunity that, he said, came "by chance."[20] Berklee records and academic catalogs do not list Cook among the faculty, suggesting that he may have served in a role as an adjunct or contracted instructor, perhaps subbing for another saxophone or jazz instructor away on tour.[21] Saxophonist Richie Cole, who attended Berklee from 1966 to 1969, noted that he had studied at Berklee with Joe Viola and with Cook after winning a scholarship to attend the school, according to an interview in *Cadence* magazine and a later *DownBeat* obituary.[22] The "Caught in the Act" section of the 6 February 1969 issue of *DownBeat* featured William Tesson's recounting of Berklee College of Music's Thursday Night Dues Band in concert at New England

Life Hall in Boston. The Thursday Night Dues Band was a student band supplemented with Berklee faculty and established players. The article noted Cook as guest soloist subbing for saxophonist and Berklee faculty Andy McGhee. The *DownBeat* article described Cook as a "Berklee colleague" of McGhee (but did not describe Cook as Berklee "faculty"). Tesson's one-liner described Cook's performance as "excellent." Accompanying the article was a Lee Tanner photograph of a smiling, dapper Cook (about 35 years of age) enveloped in shadow and holding his tenor round his neck and a cigarette in his hand. The immersive shadow and rising wisp of smoke from Cook's cigarette invokes the 1948 photo of saxophone great Dexter Gordon at the Royal Roost club in New York City. (Tesson notes prophetically that many of the student performances were "unquestionably on a professional level" and that the program "augured well for the future" of the student musicians in the band. Indeed, the "reeds" included then-Berklee students Richard "Richie" Cole and Bill Pierce.)[23]

Saxophonist Bill Pierce remembered Cook on the Berklee scene and also recalled Berklee, as an institution, as more of a continuing education environment. Berklee College of Music, by Pierce's memory, was not the type of school (as it is now) where students would enroll fresh out of high school. Berklee Professor Larry Baione similarly recalled that Berklee hosted students of older age during the 1960s; military musicians would enroll at Berklee to study music using GI Bill benefits following their military service. Other students might enroll in a traditional college or university and, deciding after one or two years that they wanted to study music instead, would pursue Berklee.[24]

Cook relayed in a 1985 interview that Berklee faculty, including Herb Pomeroy, Charlie Mariano, and Jaki Byard, had invited Cook to teach and take classes at Berklee since he had relocated to Boston and, at that time, was not traveling as much for gigs. The arrangement was a "pretty free situation," by Cook's account, who elaborated that he conducted jazz workshops at the school, where students would bring their compositions to play and receive feedback. Cook also took arranging and composition courses himself, just eager to be around the music and to continue learning. Cook, in the interview with broadcaster Kamman, expressed a satisfaction and a certain reward from being able to invest in younger players with his experience and help them over their first "hurdles" in pursuit of a career in music.[25] Cook may have found a similar outlet to invest in young musicians and guide their development when he immersed himself in the New York City jam scene about a decade later in clubs like the Star Café and Augie's.

Landry also cherished the memory of Cook's devotion to his students. A Berklee student visited Cook at their apartment one day. When the student asked Cook to define an octave, Cook put his horn to his mouth and played the song "Over the Rainbow," the first two notes of which are an octave apart from one another (aligning with the lyrics, "Some-where . . ."). Cook played the song magnificently, according to Landry, and then he chuckled and told the student, "If you want to know what an octave is, learn to play 'Over the Rainbow.'"[26]

Cook also pursued gigs in the Boston area, including concerts (as the Junior Cook Quartet) at Fenway Park (Fens Stadium) on 18 May 1968, a May Jazz Happening sponsored by the Parks and Recreation Department for the City of Boston, and concerts for the Jazzwagon, a summer concert series in Boston that, by name alone, appeared to be a variation of New York City's Jazzmobile concert series, which was established four years earlier in 1964.[27]

Art Blakey and the Jazz Messengers

A number of musicians, including Pierce, expressed some surprise that Cook was never tapped to join Art Blakey's iconic Jazz Messengers. Only one documented instance of Cook pairing with Art Blakey has been discovered to date. Cook, though not formally part of the ensemble, sat in with the Blakey group during a performance at the Jazz Workshop in Boston, Massachusetts, on 20 and 21 August 1970. The timing aligns with accounts of Cook residing in Boston and being affiliated with Berklee College of Music circa 1970, just before he joined Freddie Hubbard's quintet. A 2023 release on Gearbox Records, *Art Blakey and the Jazz Messengers: Live at the Jazz Workshop 1970*, features Cook sharing the stage on one recorded song, "East of the Sun," on soprano saxophone. Andy Bey doles out his vocals patiently like wartime rations, while Cook just as patiently follows the song form, mildly embellishing the melody for one chorus. Through Gearbox's apologetically lo-fi recording of "historical importance," Blakey appears to say at the end of the track, "I could do this all day."

While the Gearbox Records vinyl only features Cook on the one track, purchase of the record allows access to a QR code inside to download additional recordings from the date and additional opportunities to experience Cook on a rare soprano outing. Those recordings include Cook on "The Theme." Ramon Morris's tenor strains toward a Coltrane-esque timbre on the rhythm changes alteration while Cook's soprano hand-dances a web of melody around Blakey's rhythms; Morris and Cook eventually take to simultaneous attack of the changes before closing the tune.

Freddie Hubbard

Cook in the late 1960s joined the quintet of trumpeter Freddie Hubbard, whose star was on the rise in the jazz world. Here again Cook's tenure with Silver and the sense of community likely brought Cook to Hubbard's attention. Recall that Hubbard, discussing the similarities between Cook and Joe Henderson, had mentioned that he and Cook played gigs together in Brooklyn nearly a decade before.

Cook joined Hubbard's quintet in the late 1960s on tenor saxophone, sometimes doubling on flute. A 3 July 1969 performance at the Newport Jazz Festival was likely among Cook's earlier gigs with Hubbard's group. The year 1970 marked the establishment of CTI Records and jazz's foray, at the hands of CTI among other record labels, into more electronic, fusion, and rock domains. Hubbard was a prominent part of CTI's lineup. One *Jazz Music Archives* web reviewer summarized the genre and Hubbard's album *Keep Your Soul Together* (CTI Records, 1973) as a pairing of "jazz fusion with a bit (or a lot) of psychedelic production," following the precedents set by Miles Davis and Herbie Hancock.[28]

Cook's association with Hubbard and, through Hubbard, with the CTI imprint marked a change in Cook's improvisational approach away from the hard bop foundations established in Silver's quintet and the Silver-less quintet with Blue Mitchell in the mid- to late 1960s. Hubbard for his part appeared to attempt to downplay those stylistic changes in some interviews. He asserted in a 1972 *DownBeat* article that the musicians on his recordings and under CTI were "still playing the same way, but the rhythm is changing, and it's drawing people into the music who didn't like it before, or couldn't relate to it."[29] Others, however, highlighted precisely that Hubbard's CTI recordings marked "a departure from the musical styles and ensemble settings of his earlier career" in favor of "characteristic" CTI studio recording production, which sought to "satisfy fans of rock, soul, and jazz music."[30] In this way, critic Simon Hunt's characterization of "Red Clay" as "stretch[ing] the hard bop textures with a new electric feel" seems an understatement.[31] A *Jazz Journal* (UK) review of *Freddie Hubbard/Stanley Turrentine: In Concert Vols 1 and 2* summarized the metamorphosis, describing Hubbard as "sounding strong and confident in his newish role as a competent purveyor of the new jazz-rock style, initiated by Miles Davis with his *Bitches Brew* release in 1969 and gathering considerable momentum by 1973."[32]

Hubbard's turn toward fusion and rock, like Miles Davis's own transition, was not without its critics. Some of the fiercest criticism came from other musicians who sought to preserve more traditional hard bop roots. The music magazine *Black Echoes* quoted drummer Louis Hayes as being "depressed to see so many gifted jazz musicians playing so far below their natural capabilities in order to leap on the dollar-earning 'bland-wagon' of so-called fusion or crossover music." Author Mike Henessey raged in the same article that jazz had been "infiltrated and adulterated by ritualized funk, mock-rock, sham-soul and electronic chicanery."[33]

The arc of Cook's playing during this period took a different turn, toward the style of John Coltrane. Several of Cook's friends and associates noted his love of Coltrane. Drummer Joe Farnsworth remembered that Cook held Coltrane in highest esteem, sometimes referring to himself as JC2, the original JC being Coltrane. Farnsworth surmised that Cook's desire was never to sound like Coltrane, but Coltrane and his example inspired Cook to travel his own creative path. More broadly, jazz producer Michael Cuscuna and other sources underscored the pervasive influence of Coltrane on jazz. For example, Cuscuna noted that in the 1960s, Coltrane released a record about every six months, and with each release he was evolving, innovating, and doing something new and impactful.[34] During a European tour years later in the 1980s, Cook connected with his friend and adoring fan Jerry Bauer and hosted him in his hotel room to listen to early Coltrane records on Cook's cassette tape player—"The one," Jerry Bauer recalled, "where you press a button at the end and the cassette would jump into the air." (When Bauer asked Cook if it was time for him to get a better tape deck, Cook replied, "For what I want to hear that's good enough.")[35]

In Cook's playing, flowing eighth notes became alternately more rhythmic jabs and faster groupings of notes. Cook's use of the altissimo register—the saxophone's highest notes, beyond the normal range of the horn—increased. His solos featured more "screams," in a manner that many have attributed to Coltrane's broad influence, both on Cook and on jazz tenors of the time. Pianist Michael Weiss also observed, in the context of Cook's time in the Hubbard quintet, that the song that a musician is playing and the repertoire that a musician is pulling from will play a role in how the musician approaches a song. The difference in Cook's improvisational approach in Hubbard's quintet versus in Silver's was as palpable as the difference between Silver's "Cookin' at the Continental" and "Señor Blues"—hard bop staples—and Hubbard's "Intrepid Fox" and "Keep Your Soul Together," which were frequently played in his jazz fusion–jazz rock concert sets.

In Weiss's observation this repertory effect was in no way limited to Cook. Stanley Turrentine's CTI outings, also with Freddie Hubbard, took a similar turn away from the bop influences of his earlier years toward a less melodic, if more emotive, approach. In much the same way that Cook's tenure with the Freddie Hubbard quintet (during Hubbard's affiliation with CTI) diverged from Cook's earlier improvisational moorings, Turrentine's CTI-era performances were not Blue Note Turrentine (reminiscent of the improvisational style or repertoire that Turrentine displayed on his Blue Note Records releases) or Three Sounds Turrentine (harking to his association with the jazz trio led by pianist Gene Harris). It's also notable that, post-CTI, both Cook and Turrentine seemed to turn back to their more traditional hard bop roots—or if not *all the way* back to their Blue Note traits, they at least let their feet off the CTI jazz-rock gas for a more traditional, flowing, melodic reference point reminiscent of their earlier recordings.

Paul Desmond, by contrast, seemed immune to that CTI effect. Ethan Iverson's review of Desmond's album *Pure Desmond* (CTI, 1975) notes that "Desmond himself is in excellent form, just like he always was."[36] Even Bob James's alternately rolling and percussive Rhodes accompaniment on *Take Ten* (RCA Victor, 1963) and Gabor Szabo's reaching guitar on Desmond's 1973 CTI album *Skylark* could scarcely coax Desmond away from his oft-quoted "dry martini" sound and style. Desmond stood firm with a sound and approach that would have been just as at home had it been lifted and shifted back in time to a *Time Out* alternate take from more than a decade prior. In other words, CTI Desmond still sounded like Desmond.

Hubbard, for his part, was riding a strong wave of critical and popular notoriety, and Cook was along for the ride. Hubbard won second place in *DownBeat* magazine's 1970 Critic's Poll in the trumpet category; Miles Davis was first.[37] Hubbard's CTI release First Light (1971) earned Hubbard the only Grammy award of his career in 1972 for Best Jazz Performance by a Group.

In Cook and Hubbard were two starkly different personalities, according to several musicians and associates of Cook. Hubbard himself in a 1973 interview alluded to Cook's personality: "With me now I have saxophonist Junior Cook, who is just beginning to get that excitement that I wanted. There was a period elapsed in between Horace Silver and me, where he became very discouraged with the scene; I had to go and get him out of Boston, bring him back to New York. Now he's kinda relaxed, and he's playing better. He's a very introverted, quiet, beautiful cat. He doesn't assert himself maybe as much as other guys; that's the reason he hasn't made that many albums."[38]

Cook's reserve was Hubbard's braggadocio. Cook's introverted demeanor was Hubbard's outright challenge to musical duels, his trumpet a three-chamber revolver. Cook's perceived lack of ambition was Hubbard's declaration that he was top of the heap. National Endowment of the Arts Jazz Master saxophonist Benny Golson described Hubbard as "provocative," daring musicians to prove their mettle on difficult or complex chord changes.[39] Saxophonist Fred Daniels, a transplant from San Francisco to

New York City in the mid-1960s, recalled Hubbard's constant barrage of superlatives for himself. One night Daniels was transporting Hubbard, Cook, and other musicians after a gig, bobbing and weaving through New York City traffic. Hubbard cautioned, "Careful! You're gonna kill the greatest trumpet player in the world!" Daniels, weary of Hubbard's bragging, responded, "Miles is not in the car."[40]

Cook toured and recorded with Hubbard during this period, including Hubbard albums *Keep Your Soul Together* and *High Energy*. The *Boston Globe* also documented Hubbard's appearance at the 1974 Newport Jazz Festival "with three well-known sidemen tenor saxophonist Junior Cook, bassist Reggie Workman, and drummer Jack DeJohnette"; this was the twenty-first running of the festival and took place at New York's Carnegie Hall. The article characterized Hubbard as "leaning toward an undisciplined music which is taking much of the bite out of his playing," having earlier characterized Hubbard as "progressive" but "primarily safe" because the "commercial success" of the group "guarantees ticket sales."[41]

Cook's time in the Hubbard unit came to an end in the mid-1970s. According to vocalist Shepherd, Cook decided that he had to move on after a period, concerned that he wouldn't grow as a musician in the Hubbard unit, which Shepherd himself characterized as "sophisticated rock and roll." As noted earlier, the repertoire and musical direction of Hubbard at that time—call it jazz rock, call it fusion—was a departure from Cook's mooring as a soloist. During a March 1973 concert in Paris captured on video, the quintet is blazing through Hubbard's "Intrepid Fox."[42] Cook appears to snipe at young drummer Michael Carvin—"Bring it down, man!" with his mouthpiece still in his mouth—at what appears to be a point where Cook is leading the quintet toward a slow simmer as he brings his solo to a close, but Carvin failed to follow, maintaining his drum rhythms at a blistering tempo and volume. It's only one observed datapoint but nonetheless may be an indicator that Cook was growing tired of the fusion push toward what journalist Ben Ratliff described as "textural music" and that he longed for the structure and definition of the bop forms in which he had earlier flourished.[43]

Another account suggested that the Hubbard unit continued to tour and perform, leaving Cook behind. Timmy Shepherd indicated that, having finished a European tour, Hubbard and his band, including Cook, had returned to the States. When Hubbard embarked on another overseas tour, Cook was left behind. In an interaction between Hubbard and Cook years later at the Star Café, Hubbard had blamed it on the industry, claiming that his record label producers insisted that he replace Cook with a "white boy on tenor," according to Shepherd's recollection.[44]

Elvin Jones Quartet

Online biographical sketches of Cook relay, often without elaboration, that he also played in an ensemble with drum legend Elvin Jones. One video on YouTube captures Cook with the Elvin Jones Quartet at the Music Inn, one of Rome's best known jazz venues, in 1975, with Roland Prince on guitar and David Williams on bass.[45] The mind almost seems to conjure up John Coltrane when one listens to a saxophonist, who is not Coltrane, playing with one of the members of Coltrane's iconic quartet. His eighth notes flow like water over a minor tune, and he sways at attention in a two-step in time with Jones's propulsive drumming during the other solos. The Trane conjuring is even easier when the second tune of the set is Coltrane's composition, "Naima." Cook starts the tune with an intro cadenza, and the song develops in a rubato form, though Cook's periodic vertical swaying on the beat—and guitarist Roland Prince's hurried chords—seem to indicate Cook's conclusion that the tune could have used more rhythmic structure.

Louis Hayes Quintet

In 1975 drummer Louis Hayes organized a band, seeking to capitalize on a lead he received for gig and touring opportunities in Europe. Pianist Cedar Walton, on his return from a European tour, relayed that a promoter in Holland (now The Netherlands) was eager to book American jazz groups on tour. Hayes secured Ronnie Mathews (piano) and Stafford James (bass), both of whom lived in Brooklyn at the time, like Hayes. Hayes called in Cook, with whom he had maintained a friendship since their time together in the late 1950s in Horace Silver's quintet before Hayes left the group to work with Cannonball Adderley. Trumpeter Woody Shaw, a young sensation in his early 30s, rounded out the group, and Maxine Gordon (née Gregg) handled the business management on the road.

The band warmed up with a few domestic gigs before taking their show abroad. As early as September 1975, the quintet was gigging at Boomer's restaurant, 340 Bleecker Street, Greenwich Village, between West Tenth and Christopher Streets in New York City ("four shows nightly starting at 9:30 pm weekdays and 10:30pm weekends," according to a writeup in the *New York Times*).[46] In October 1975 the quintet performed at Baltimore's Famous Ballroom, followed by another stint at Boomer's in Greenwich Village in the first quarter of 1976. Shortly thereafter the band—billed as the Louis Hayes–Junior Cook Quintet or the Louis Hayes–Junior Cook Quintet, featuring Woody Shaw—took a round of dates in Europe, including Belgium, Germany, and Austria. The band departed the States in 1976 for a European tour, organized by concert promoter Wim Wigt and his company Wim Wigt Productions. Maxine Gordon, road manager for the group, relayed the fun and logistical precision of maintaining schedules and managing travel from one performance to the next.[47] The band would often travel by train among European cities, filling a passenger suite with Stafford James's acoustic bass splayed across overhead luggage racks, each end resting on opposite sides of the compartment. Disembarking could be a challenge, as the trains often only spent a few minutes at each station for passengers to board or to depart and required the band members to pass the instruments out the window of the train to ensure all equipment was offloaded.

The band carried on the legacy and flame of the hard-driving, uncompromising hard bop groups of the previous decades, including Art Blakey's Jazz Messengers and the Horace Silver quintets. Hayes said of the group: "We could just knock people out because it [the music] was so strong."[48] *DownBeat* magazine chronicled the quintet's performance at Howard University's Cramton Auditorium as part of the Left Bank Jazz Society of DC Festival in 1976. The Hayes–Cook quintet opened the show with Woody Shaw's composition "Moontrane," a staple of the quintet's performance set, and the article described "their ensemble work" as "flawless" as "each player turned in substantial solos before the set was over." "Junior Cook's

Original chord changes for the first eight measures of Kerns' "All the Things You Are."

bright tenor was challenging throughout, and particularly effective on Monk's 'Pannonica,'" the article continued, calling the unit a "well-balanced quintet."[49] Only two months later, *DownBeat*, again in its "Caught" segment of concert performances, described the Woody Shaw–Louis Hayes Quintet and its performance at the Village Vanguard. Dubbing the quintet's style "neo-bop," writer Chuck Berg lauded the quintet's performance, this time with Rene McLean on tenor, rather than Cook. Berg concluded that "1977 should be a very good year for the quintet," citing as evidence the release of the *Ichi-Ban* album on Timeless records—a project released under the Louis Hayes–Junior Cook Quintet moniker and featuring Cook, not McLean, in the tenor chair.[50] Another article in the same *DownBeat* issue (page 11) heralded Dexter Gordon's triumphant return to the United States, highlighting that Gordon was supported by "the rhythm section from Woody Shaw's new group," referring to (at that point in time, post-Cook) the Hayes–Shaw quintet.[51]

Contrasting with the Hubbard group, the Hayes–Cook quintet returned to solid bop territory. Whereas some of Hubbard's repertoire—including "First Light," "Intrepid Fox," "Little Sunflower," and "Keep Your Soul Together"—lay into grooves, in many instances with minimal chords, the Hayes–Cook quintet faced the opposite direction, doubling down on harmonically complex modern classics, like Woody Shaw's "Moontrane," but also revisiting established jazz classics with harmonic substitutions. Jerome Kern's "All the Things You Are" is an example in this regard: the Hayes–Cook quintet tackled this jazz standard with gusto, incorporating tritone substitutions and other harmonic deviations to make the improvisations more intricate and interesting. In so doing, they also challenged the notion that hard bop as a rule lacked harmonic sophistication or the bebop-era virtuosity necessary to navigate intricate chord changes.

These first eight measures of "All the Things You Are" illustrate the harmonic substitutions (in measures three and four) frequently reflected in Cook's improvisational approach to the song.

The Hayes–Cook quintet's 1976 recording highlights Cook firmly under the influence of Coltrane. The approach also is likely a product of the collective intensity of the band's personnel, which included Louis Hayes on drums and the explosive Woody Shaw on trumpet. Cook's higher note frequency ("higher," as in he played more notes), altissimo explorations, and incorporation of more intricate harmonic paths all were on display in his outings with the Hayes quintet. Cook also can be heard again interspersing his longer, melodic lines with Coltrane-influenced shorter phrases—what biographer Ben Ratliff refers to as the "babbling, short-phrase Coltrane, the full-strength incantatory of 'Chasin' the Trane.'"[52] German author, jazz critic, and pianist Baldur Bockhoff, reviewing a Hayes–Cook quintet concert in March 1976, described Woody Shaw's phrases as "always cleanly formulated" and "logical," "nothing is botched." On the other hand, Bockhoff asserted that Cook "reverses Shaw's logic," elaborating that Cook's solos were "teeming with passages, reflections" with little "linear clarity": "No wonder that he [Cook] initially explores a ballad in free rhapsodizing and only occasionally leaves a familiar tree standing when there is a striking harmonic turn."[53]

Cook, however, was not one to dismiss or jettison his past associations (Silver, Mitchell, Hubbard) but, rather, built upon them. The album *Louis Hayes/Junior Cook Quintet: At Onkel Po's Carnegie Hall, Hamburg 1976*, for example, features Cook on an emotive and urgent rendition of Mancini and Mercer's "Moment to Moment." Hubbard had recorded the tune five years earlier for his masterpiece *First Light* album (CTI, 1971), for which he won a Grammy award in 1972.

Perhaps Cook's laid-back style, or perhaps his inattention to the business side of the music business, contributed to his decision to cut ties with the quintet after about a year. The circumstances seem to point toward conflict between Cook and Shaw. Timmy Shepherd relayed hearing from Cook himself that the Hayes–Cook quintet, touring Europe, had arrived in Paris for a performance date to find the marquee advertising the Louis Hayes–Woody Shaw Quintet rather than the Louis Hayes–Junior Cook Quintet, the name under which the band had been established.[54] In fact, a schedule of upcoming Paris concerts in the February 1976 issue of *Jazz Hot* magazine listed the quintet's 6 February 1976 concert at Nouveau Carré as "le quintette de Louis Hayes avec Woody Shaw," and the following month the magazine listed "le Louis Hayes/Junior Cook Quintet" in concert at the same venue on 31 March 1976.[55] Other musicians, with whom Cook discussed the matter, recount that the change of marquee billing for that February 1976 gig had greatly upset Cook. According to those accounts, Cook went to a restaurant for dinner that evening and penned his resignation letter from the group. Asked in 2022 about the circumstances of Cook's departure from the group, Hayes himself declined to answer, saying it was personal for him and he preferred to "keep that to [himself]." Hayes did offer that, though he and Cook "grew apart" as a band, they did not grow apart personally and had remained friends.[56]

Woody Shaw III, in the liner notes for a 2017 two-volume CD release of the quintet's music from 1976 and 1977 on the High Note Record label (*Volume One*, 2016; *Volume Two*, 2017), noted that "Cook's departure from the (Hayes-Cook) group . . . resulted from a little skirmish between Woody and Junior."[57] An article in the 2 October 1976 issue of the UK music magazine *Melody Maker* elaborated on that "skirmish" following the quintet's gig at Ronnie Scott's jazz club in London. The article, entitled "Woody Shaw: The Intimidator," suggests a fight between Shaw and Cook just the night before: "Woody Shaw didn't look much like The Intimidator. A slight, long limbed man in his early thirties with a permanent deep crease in his brow, he looked deceptively mild. Until, that is, one examined his right hand, where most of the skin was ripped from the knuckles, the result of a 'disagreement' with his former colleague, tenorist Junior Cook the night before [1 October 1976]."[58] Shaw himself, in a *DownBeat* interview, mentioned that the Louis Hayes–led band had a "strong thing" musically while also highlighting that he had "some personal conflicts with Junior Cook."[59] *DownBeat* magazines as early as 4 November 1976, barely a month after the Ronnie Scott's gig, advertised the Louis Hayes and Woody Shaw group at the Jazz Showcase in

Chicago (17–21 November 1976) and at the Tralfamodore Café in Buffalo (3–5 December 1976). Cook, who played a key role in what *DownBeat* in October 1976 had called "flawless" ensemble work, was no longer on the quintet's roster. By the late 1970s Cook was back in New York City, ready for his next band adventure.

In 1979 Cook recorded with trumpeter Louis Smith on the latter's leader recording, entitled *Prancin'*, for SteepleChase records, yet another example of Cook's durable network of musicians forged over decades of playing. Recall that Cook and Smith fronted the Silver Quintet before Blue Mitchell joined the group, performing at the Newport Jazz Festival concert in 1958. Flanked by a rhythm section of Roland Hanna (piano), Sam Jones (bass), and Billy Hart (drums), Cook and Smith champion the mostly medium-tempo session of mostly Smith compositions, reigniting some Silver-esque song intros and unique two-measure tags to cue up instrumental solos on songs like "One for Nils." Cook, as per usual, weaves a sonic tapestry through the changes with a focus that spotlights his maturity at executing money-note melodies with child's-play ease.

Bill Hardman

The Bill Hardman–Junior Cook Quintet was a late 1970s and 1980s iteration of a band personnel structure—the classic quintet with trumpet and tenor saxophone on the front line—with a gravitational pull that Cook seemed almost unable to resist. The quintet setting—fronting bands with Blue Mitchell (both in the Horace Silver group and in Mitchell's own), Freddie Hubbard, Woody Shaw (in the Hayes–Cook quintet), and then with Hardman—seemed to be a formula that worked best for Cook. The Hardman–Cook band quickly endeared itself to musicians and music lovers alike. John Wilson in the *New York Times* described Hardman and Cook as leading a quintet that "epitomizes the character and colors of the hard-bop era," and the *New York Times* obituary for Bill Hardman called his quintet with Junior Cook "adventurous" and "groundbreaking."[60]

The Hardman–Cook quintet was established toward the end of 1978. The group at its start featured Hardman on trumpet, Cook on tenor, Mickey

Tucker or Ronnie Mathews on piano, Yoshio "Chin" Suzuki on bass, and Leroy Williams on drums. Hardman and his wife, Roseline, resided in a Brooklyn apartment and had secured the apartment next door to use as music studio or guest lodging. Hardman was well-known from his stint with Art Blakey and the Jazz Messengers; the pairing of Hardman and Cook—both accomplished musicians in their own right and both alumni of seminal hard bop groups—in one powerhouse quintet set the music scene on fire. The Hardman–Cook quintet was the "talk of the town among musicians," according to SteepleChase Records founder Nils Winther.[61] Jazz drummer Joe Farnsworth pegged the Hardman–Cook quintet as "the last of the real true hard bop groups."[62]

The Hardman–Cook quintet came to play. The band members each are remembered for a high level of technical proficiency on their respective instruments and aural retention without the benefit of sheet music. The quintet was regarded as "the people's band," and they drew a constant and faithful following.[63] In one anecdote the Hardman–Cook quintet secured a gig at the Village Gate in Greenwich Village, opening for Cuban jazz woodwind virtuoso Paquito D'Rivera. D'Rivera had released his first solo album, *Paquito Blowin'*, on Columbia Records in 1981 and a decade later would perform as a regular with Dizzy Gillespie and his United Nations Orchestra. The crowds converged at the Village Gate to hear the Hardman–Cook quintet and then departed before D'Rivera's set. The next night, the order reportedly was switched. D'Rivera was scheduled to play first, ostensibly to pin down the Hardman–Cook crowd for both shows, but the Hardman-Cook quintet faithful arrived at the club only in time to catch the later show.[64] The Hardman–Cook group also scored gigs at the Flamingo Lounge on Eastern Parkway in Brooklyn, Pumpkins in Crown Heights, and at the Val Hal Club.

The "people's band" must be accessible to the people, and the Jazzmobile concert series (Jazzmobile, Inc.), founded in 1964, was just the mechanism for that purpose.[65] SteepleChase founder Nils Winther heard Cook several times in New York as part of the Jazzmobile series of concerts, and Winther had sought out Cook and asked him to record for SteepleChase on the strength of his Jazzmobile performances and from having heard Cook on Louis Smith's

1979 SteepleChase recording, *Prancin'*. A *New York Times* article in 1976 noted that the "audiences are mainly New Yorkers who don't regularly go to Carnegie or Town or Avery Fisher Halls," continuing in the same article that Jazzmobile audiences are made up of some music fans "but are mostly street people." The article described the Jazzmobile operation as follows:

> A pickup truck towing a flatbed trailer with a black and white bandstand comes to a stop on an Upper Manhattan street, microphones and other sound paraphernalia are set up, musicians mount the stand, a few announcements are made and suddenly the sound of jazz floats through the area.
>
> Children bounce rhythmically in front of the stand. Older persons drift to the site and, caught up by the music, begin tapping their feet and snapping their fingers.
>
> The Jazzmobile is on the scene.[66]

Jazzmobile shows were big events throughout New York: in Manhattan, Queens, Brooklyn, and the Bronx. Some concerts were set in parks—Grant's Tomb was an especially sought-after gig—and sometimes set on random streets; Jazzmobile in mid-July 1983 presented the Johnny Griffin quartet in concert at 132nd Street between Adam Clayton Powell Boulevard and Lenox Avenue, for example, and the Hardman–Cook quintet performed the following week at St. Nicholas Avenue, between 112th and 113th Streets.[67]

Jazzmobile was a pick-up block party. Community organizations throughout New York City could request a Jazzmobile concert. People brought lawn chairs, drinks, and even their grills to make the most of the concert experience. Concertgoers might catch sight of Kareem Abdul Jabar, Bill Cosby, Debbie Allen, boxers, and other athletes out to enjoy the music. Hardman was called often to schedule the one- or two-hour Jazzmobile concerts for the quintet because of the positive public reception to the group's driving, no-nonsense musical momentum. Timmy Shepherd recalled, "Cats were dancing in the streets to 'Moment's Notice.' I've never seen anything like it!"[68]

The Hardman–Cook unit brought the same fire overseas. A review of a Hardman–Cook quintet performance at Ronnie Scott's jazz club in London underscored the group dynamic, frontline sympatico between the horns, and individual virtuosity among the members. Reviewer Mike Hennessey said that the musicians in the unit had little chance of "finishing up the jazz hall of fame as great innovators" but lauded the "good, honest musicianship and conviction" among the players. Of Cook Hennessey wrote, "Any saxophone player who has the epic Sonny Rollins/John Coltrane *Tenor Madness* locked into his consciousness, as Junior Cook does," had the reviewer's full attention. He described Cook's solos as "thoughtful, constructive, and side-stepping cliches with commendable flair" and summarized that the unit's musicians to a man were "fine musicians . . . whose celebrity falls so far short of their skills."[69] Pianist Michael Weiss, who played in the quintet following Tucker's departure, shared the schedule of the group's (Hardman, Cook, Weiss, Walter Booker [bass], Leroy Williams [drums]) extensive tour of Europe in 1986:[70]

Performance Date	Venue	City/Country
September 24	New Morning	Paris, France
September 25	Riverside Jazzclub	Antwerp, Belgium
September 26	Bimhuis	Amsterdam, The Netherlands
September 27	Domicil	Dortmund, West Germany
September 29	Birdland	Hamburg, West Germany
September 30	Quasimodo	Berlin, West Germany
October 1	Quasimodo	Berlin, West Germany
October 3	Mahogany Hall	Edam, The Netherlands
October 4–5	Topos	Leverkusen, DE
October 6	Cafetaria des Jubez	Karlsruhe, DE
October 7–9	Jazzland	Vienna, Austria
October 10	Brucknerhaus	Linz, Austria
October 11	Scharfrichterhaus	Passau, Austria
October 12	Domicile	Munich, DE
October 13–16	Widderbar	Zurich, Switzerland
October 18	Teatro Sperimentali	Ancona, Italy
October 19	Capolinea	Milano, Italy

(*Continued*)

Continued

Performance Date	Venue	City/Country
October 20	Auditorium RAI	Torino, Italy
October 22	Disco-TV	Zagreb, Yugoslavia (now Croatia)

Cook also booked gigs of his own interspersed within the schedule of the quintet with Hardman and special guest appearances with other headliners. Musicians recalled hearing Cook-led groups at the Tin Palace in New York City, as well as at Sweet Basil's and the Village Vanguard. While New York City was by far Cook's base of operations, he ventured beyond New York's boundaries occasionally. *The Washington Post* chronicled periodic doses of Cook leading a quartet throughout the 1980s at the iconic One Step Down, a now-shuttered DC jazz club on Pennsylvania Avenue NW, just outside Georgetown and in the shadow of Columbia Hospital for Women. Cook performed at the club often on Fridays and Saturdays. He appeared at the One Step with Gene Adler (piano), Ed Howard (bass), and Lenny Robinson (drums) in December 1987; Rueben Brown (piano), Geoff Harper (bass), and Steve Williams (drums) in December 1989; and Larry Willis (piano), Ed Howard (bass), and Steve Williams (drums) in January 1991. He also appeared at the One Step in September 1985 as part of the Nat Adderley quintet, which also featured Larry Willis (piano), Walter Booker (bass), and Jimmy Cobb (drums).

Ad for Junior Cook at the One Step Down, 4–5 January 1991. *Washington Post*, 4 January 1991, p. 17.

Cook's out-of–New York City gigs still were mostly on the Eastern seaboard, with a quartet of his own or as a featured artist playing with a local house band. A sampling of gig venues included: the Cornerstone in Metuchen, New Jersey, with the Michael Weiss Quartet, featuring Cook (1985); the Artist's Quarter, Minneapolis, Minnesota (1985); the Gaslight Inn, Mt. Holly, New Jersey (1987); Jazz Club 2080, Montreal, Canada, with guitarist Mike Gauthier and others (late 1980s); the African American History and Cultural Museum, Philadelphia, Pennsylvania, with the Philadelphia Jazz All-Stars (1990); the 880 Club in Hartford, Connecticut, with the Don DePalma trio (1990); the Hyatt Regency, Princeton, New Jersey, for a Battle of the Tenors featuring Cook and Jerome Richardson (1990); and the Polo Bay Room of the Warwick Hotel, Philadelphia, Pennsylvania (1991). Cook played tenor in an octet led by trumpeter Howard McGee in the 1980s, according to saxophonist Henry Threadgill, and also sat in with drummer Terri Lyne Carrington in June 1982 for New York City area gigs.[71] In 1989 Cook was part of an all-star, multiday lineup celebrating the fiftieth anniversary of the Blue Note record label at Los Angeles's Ford Theatre in Hollywood in what *Cadence* magazine described as a music marathon over three successive Sundays.[72] Cook performed in an early May 1990 memorial service for tenor legend Dexter Gordon following his death the previous month.[73] On 28 June 1991 Cook again paid homage to Gordon, joining an ambitious JVC Jazz Festival tribute that included dramatic readings, tap dance, excerpts from the movie *'Round Midnight*, and ensemble performances at Lincoln Center's Avery Fisher Hall. *The Star Ledger* declared the production "too diffuse and meandering" and claimed that Cook was "mismatched with a sentimental ballad" when he played "The End of a Love Affair."[74]

Further afield, Canadian pianist and drummer Andre White also remembered Cook as one of the US jazz stars who would gig in Montreal with local rhythm sections. White played drums behind Cook in April 1982 at "Club des Musiciens, a bar inside the building that housed the Musicians Union headquarters, local 406," also known as Club 406. The band also featured Fred Henke on piano and Randy Phillips on bass. White recalled Cook "counted off the tunes the old way, by stomping—'one—two—one two three four'—with his foot on the bandstand." As if reading from the script of Cook's life, White described Cook as "a man of few words" but noted his warm appreciation—"Thanks man!"—and a hug after the gig. White's conclusion of Cook: "A serious improviser, searching on his horn, pushing himself, deep inside the changes . . . always trying to play new stuff every chance he got, sometimes successfully, sometimes not, but always courageously."[75]

Vocalist Shepherd also recalled that Cook performed alongside other musical heavyweights in an annual benefit concert for the Jackie Robinson Foundation in Stamford, Connecticut. Baseball great Jackie Robinson and his wife, Rachel, presented an all-star concert, An Afternoon in Jazz, starting in 1963 in the backyard of their Stamford home. The concert served as a benefit to raise money for civil rights activities, including bail money for student protesters.[76] The concerts continued long after Robinson's death in 1972. During one such concert (year unspecified, but based on Shepherd's association with Cook, likely in the mid-1980s), the lineup included saxophonists Frank Wess, Frank Foster, Cook, and Grover Washington Jr. Shepherd recalled that Washington had such respect for the other musicians that he played soprano saxophone for the concert that night, adamant that he did not want to go on stage and "look like a fool" playing tenor in the presence of jazz tenor saxophone giants like Foster, Wess, and Cook.[77]

Cook also presided over a 1980s jam session at a Manhattan club called the Star Café, on Twenty-Third Street near Seventh Avenue. A dive among dives with a pool table in the middle of the floor, pianist David Hazeltine remembered the Star Café as a "funky little bar" where the musicians would have to move the pool table out of the way before the jam session sets began. Hazeltine played keys for the jam on his Fender Rhodes, which he hauled in on jam nights until the Café managed to secure a spinet piano. The jam session would alternate with pool during the course of the night: The first hour was pool; during the second hour the pool table would trade places with the piano for the jam; next hour, pool; and so on. Pianist Tardo Hammer remembered the Star Café spinet piano as being "awful" but slightly more in tune than the equally awful baby grand piano at Brooklyn's Flamingo Lounge, which was owned by a "numbers guy" who wore a cowboy hat and charged three times the price for watered down drinks because there was live jazz in the room.[78] Completing the "seedy jazz bar" scene straight out of a movie set, Hazeltine's recollection of the Star Café included Little Louie, "the muscle of the club," who carried a pistol tucked in his pants. Tenorist Ralph Moore, who described the Star Café as a "bucket of blood," remembered the mismatched tables and chairs, a Black man nicknamed Rabbi, a club regular who wore a black skull cap, and an arcade machine marking the Star Café decor.[79] The Star Café also had a basement, where "things" were going on, according to Hammer (implying illicit drug activity); he never went to the Star Café basement and credited the decision with extending his lifespan. Drummer Harold White was in charge of the Star Café jam and put the bands together; Cook, trombonist Curtis Fuller, and trumpeter Brian Lynch often formed the front line. Moore recalled that Brian Lynch brought him to the Star Café; Moore and Lynch formed the front line for Horace Silver's quintet in the early 1980s. Moore formed an instant bond with Cook over their mutual association with Horace Silver's quintet, as Cook had held the same chair twenty-some years before. Moore frequented the jam, subbing for Cook when he couldn't make it. Hazeltine remembered an "abundance of tenor players . . . twenty, thirty tenor players lined up, waiting to play."[80]

Why did Cook attend the Star Café jam session so faithfully? For Cook and the rest of the core band, it was a gig like any other of the time. Hazeltine recalled the core band getting paid less than $100 for the night, so there was no less an economic imperative than any other gig.

Aside from that, the music was the imperative of the jam session—the making, the learning, the continuity through the building of community. The music was the only imperative for those musicians outside the core band, those who would come to the jam for the chance to sit in and play a few tunes with the core ensemble. The jam session was the musician's gymnasium, to maintain/tone one's musical muscles and to build additional musical muscle mass. The jam session was a gallery-walk for the ears, where players could hear the masters and contemporaries in their element playing extant repertoire, standards, and transfer knowledge, licks, and concepts from one musician to another.

By and large, the jam session was not a place where original compositions were called; the point of the jam was for the musicians to play common tunes known to all, or most. Sometimes, the calling of more complex, intricate tunes (Horace Silver's "Quicksilver," Benny Golson's

"Stablemates," Bud Powell's "Dance of the Infidels") might cull the crowd and separate the more experienced players from the novices. Thus, learning tunes and having a vast knowledge of standards was key. The jam session was a laboratory of praxis, a venue to operationalize those concepts that the musician had been perfecting and exploring all day in private, honoring the tradition in which bebop was constructed at Minton's Playhouse in Harlem and Clark Monroe's Uptown House in the 1940s.[81] The jam session also was a musical public square to meet one's heroes, to hear their stories, and to network with musicians who might call you for their next gig. (Recall that Cook first met Horace Silver when both sat in on a Lou Donaldson gig in Washington, DC.)

The jam became Cook's classroom as he interacted with younger players and imparted, by example, the wisdom of his experience in the music. Younger players frequenting the Star Café jam session included Joe Albany (piano), Benny Green (piano), David Hazeltine (piano), Ed Howard (bass), Brian Lynch (trumpet), Ralph Moore (saxophone), Ned Otter (saxophone), Rob Schneiderman (piano), Richie Vitale (trumpet), and Michael Weiss (piano). Cook later performed a similar role at a jam at Augie's jazz club, a "funky little neighborhood haunt" on the Upper West Side, sharing the stage with Joe Farnsworth on drums and Peter Bernstein on guitar.[82]

Cook's presence at the Star Café also was a draw for established musicians to visit the jam. Pianists Michael Weiss and Tardo Hammer recalled seeing the likes of Lou Donaldson (saxophone), Sonny Fortune (saxophone), Cecil Payne (saxophone), Ralph Penland (drums), Pharaoh Sanders (saxophone), Cecil Taylor (piano), Bucky Thorpe (trumpet), and Tommy Turrentine (trumpet) at the club.[83]

* * * * *

Cook's alcohol consumption likely contributed to the decline of his health and ultimately his death at the young age of 57. Cook drank as much as a fifth of Smirnoff vodka, sometimes each day. Cook suffered from what probably amounted to alcohol tremors, commonly known to some as "the shakes." The shakes sometimes would prevent Cook from being able to drink from a glass, requiring some engineering to accomplish the basic task.

Cook sometimes would be forced to tie one end of a long scarf around his wrist, loop the scarf around his neck, grab the other end of the scarf with his free hand, and pull the scarf as a makeshift pulley to raise his hand and drinking glass to his mouth.

Cook's gradual physical weakness at least in part prompted his invitation to vocalist Timmy Shepherd to room with him at his Washington Heights apartment in New York City. Cook lived at 651 W. 188th Street, near 188th and Wadsworth, apartment #6C. Shepherd shared the apartment with Cook in the mid-1980s, from about 1983 to 1987, and paid about $260 a month in rent. As Cook's effective right hand, Shepherd helped Cook get to gigs on time, often carrying his horn for him as his health declined.

Shepherd met Cook in Washington, DC, around 1979. Shepherd heard Cook on a gig at the One Step Down. At the time Cook was working with Harold White. Shepherd, a Baltimore native, later moved to New York City on the invitation of trombonist Curtis Fuller. One day Shepherd got lost on the subway and saw Cook on the same train. Cook offered to help Shepherd get to his destination, and their friendship emerged from that meeting. Cook also tutored Shepherd, who didn't read music at the time: ii-V-I progressions, familiarity with the piano, whole tones and diminished scales opened many harmonic possibilities for Shepherd.

Shepherd's son, Kelly, also knew Cook well from the association with his father. The young Shepherd recalled gifting Cook an answering machine during a gig Cook was playing at Bradley's. Kelly took the answering machine to Cook's apartment and set it up for him. Cook was very appreciative, noting after a short period of time, "I didn't know how many gigs I was missing!"[84]

Cook at some point in the 1980s began to see Beatrice Henellin, identified in Cook's *New York Times* obituary as his "companion." Cook and Henellin saw each other about twice a week, often at gigs and concerts, which she frequented. When the Hardman–Cook quintet kicked off a gig, Cook, knowing that the first few tunes would be instrumentals, tasked Timmy Shepherd to roam the audience to spot if Henellin was present. Cook and Beatrice—"Bea" as many friends remembered her—enjoyed one another's company, and she would join Cook on visits to the Hardmans' or to the Tuckers' homes. Roseline Hardman remembered Cook and Henellin as very much in love.

In 1984 Cook returned to Pensacola, Florida, to be honored in his hometown. Saxophonist Joe Evans relayed in his book, *Follow Your Heart*, that he, Cook, pianist Donald Shirley, saxophonist Thomas Gryce, and university bandleader Leander Kirksey all were inducted into the Music Makers Hall of Fame at its fourth annual celebration 6–8 July 1984; several other musicians were also honored, including Ann Gailey, former organist at Pensacola's Saenger Theater; jazz pianist Betty Moran; trumpeter and bandleader Roy Russell; and vocalist and guitarist Slim Gaillard in an induction ceremony at Pensacola's Knights of Columbus Hall.[85] Evans noted that each received the award and had an opportunity to speak about his or her career.[86]

Horace Silver's album *Music to Ease Your Disease* (Silverto Records, 1988), reunited Silver and Cook again, and also featured Clark Terry (trumpet), Ray Drummond (bass), Billy Hart (drums), and Andy Bey (vocals). With the exception of the vocals (which were comparatively rare in Silver's earlier recordings), the set list for *Music to Ease Your Disease* was a classic representation of Silver's compositional style: blues/funk, intros, outros, shout choruses. Cook contributed one-chorus solos on the songs "The Respiratory Story," "The Philanthropic View," and "What Is the Sinus Minus." Silver oddly neglected to cite Cook's participation on that album in his autobiography. Silver highlights his five albums of new music in the 1980s, starting with *Guides to Growing Up* (1981) and ending with *Music to Ease Your Disease* (1988), but he only mentioned tenor saxophonists Eddie Harris and Ralph Moore as participating on those projects.[87] Cook supports Silver's vision on this album just as authentically as on the albums of the late 1950s and early 1960s that launched his career. Cook connects with Clark Terry to deliver melodies and shout choruses with authority with remarkable two-horn-one-sound sympatico. Cook's loose-eighth-note solos meander through Silver's changes with aplomb, entwining new melodic motifs with characteristic blues inflections and wide-interval command of his horn.

The Hardmans relocated to France in August 1988, seeking security and a French education for their daughter, Nadege. Bill Hardman, however, "shared his life between New York City and Paris," according to Roseline Hardman.

The Hardmans kept an apartment in Brooklyn, and the Hardman–Cook quintet continued until Hardman's death in December 1990.

Shortly after the Hardmans' departure for Europe, in 1989 Hardman–Cook quintet pianist Mickey Tucker departed the New York–New Jersey area and relocated to Australia in a scene straight out of a movie thriller. Tucker moved to Australia (his wife is Australian) following threats on his life after witnessing what he described as a policeman involved in a mob murder of two women. Tucker's friend, Robert "Skeet" Douglas, was framed for the murder, by Tucker's telling, and Tucker's eyewitness account could have overturned the case against Douglas. Tucker's friends and associates, some connected with law enforcement, advised Tucker that his choices were to leave the country or "end up in a boneyard."[88] The Hardmans' and Tuckers' exit meant that Cook's close circle of friends, from whom he gathered strength of personal relationship and camaraderie, had diminished sharply and rapidly.

Bill and Roseline Hardman's departure from the United States to live in Paris, France, also was quite possibly a financial blow to Cook, who benefited from the quintet's active performance schedule. In the 1980s Bill Hardman was the business mind behind the Bill Hardman–Junior Cook Quintet and had organized the concerts and tours.[89]

Cook's 1980s roommate and right hand, Timmy Shepherd, described another instance of Cook's apparent lack of business acumen and how it hurt him over time. The anecdote finds Cook, Curtis Fuller, Cedar Walton, and Freddie Hubbard slated to perform together at a party to celebrate the jazz film *'Round Midnight.* Released in 1986, the film was inspired by the story of Frenchman Francis Paudras, who had befriended Bud Powell, jazz pianist and architect, along with Dizzy Gillespie, Charlie Parker, and others of the bebop style of jazz. Director Bertrand Tavernier cast real-life tenor legend Dexter Gordon in the lead role as expatriate jazz musician Dale Turner, a character loosely based on jazz tenor saxophone player Lester Young and Powell. Cook asked Curtis Fuller how much money the musicians were earning for the date, and Fuller responded that each musician must negotiate his own fee. According to one account of the story, Cook negotiated a $500 fee for the date, and he was dismayed to learn later that Fuller and

Hubbard each had secured $1,500 paychecks for the same gig.[90] Another account of the same incident relayed the same basic outline but claimed the payouts were $1,000 for Cook and $10,000 each for the other musicians that night.[91] The figures vary but the constant in the two accounts of the story, both reportedly relayed directly from Cook, is the claim that Cook had earned much less compensation for the same gig. Cook's friends communicated his sense of hurt that the other musicians seemingly had distanced themselves from him; there was little sense of "we're in this together" or "let's make sure we all are taken care of." While dedicated to his craft and to making his living and career as a jazz musician, Cook was not aggressive as a leader and, as this and other instances suggest, not aggressive enough in the business of the music.

Close friends also observed Hardman's relocation to France as an emotional blow to Cook, who took Hardman's move very hard. Roseline Hardman said Bill and Junior were "like brothers," and Shepherd described them as two men with one spirit. Roseline Hardman surmised that Bill's death, of a cerebral hemorrhage on 6 December 1990 at age 57, "destroyed" Junior. In Hardman, Cook had found a human connection. They fronted the Hardman-Cook quintet and shared the same thoughts and desires about the music and how it should be respected. Shepherd drew the same conclusion as Roseline Hardman: "When Bill died, I think Junior died."[92]

During this period Cook pulled another pickup gig with yet more heavy-hitting, original voices in jazz. Continuing his personal tour through the iconic quartet of John Coltrane, Cook participated in the McCoy Tyner big band in the late 1980s and early 1990s. A big band to match and amplify McCoy Tyner's own driving, emotive piano voice is almost too much to imagine. Cook's fluid, melodic solos float characteristically over the changes on "Three Flowers" and "Uptown" on Tyner's *Uptown/Downtown: Live at the Blue Note* album. Tyner's *Turning Point* album, recorded in November 1991 and released after Cook's death, continued the driving, aural tour de force, with an all-star cast that included Cook, Frank Lacy and Steve Turre (trombones), and John Stubblefield on tenor saxophone, among others, with arrangements by Slide Hampton and Dennis Mackrel.

AGREED TO AND ACCEPTED:

by Junior Cook
Junior Cook

address:

651 W. 88th st
#6C
10040 NY, NY

Junior Cook's signature and address from the SteepleChase Records contract for his quartet recording on 27 June 1989 at A&R Studio, NYC. Material from this session was released as *On a Misty Night* on the SteepleChase label. Courtesy of Nils Winther.

Cook also took on a tenor saxophone chair and, occasionally, baritone saxophone in the Clifford Jordan big band. Jordan and Cook both were signed to the Riverside jazz label in the early 1960s but did not have occasion to collaborate at that time.[93] Jordan and Cook recorded together less than a decade earlier on the album *Two Tenor Winner* (Criss Cross, 1984), and twenty-five some years prior, Cook's long association with Horace Silver started as a replacement for Jordan in 1958. The album *Play What You Feel*, released on the Mapleshade label four years before Jordan's death, was recorded live at Condon's Jazz Club in late December 1990. Cook took tenor duties on the date and shifted to baritone saxophone for some road gigs, according to sax tech Roberto Romeo of Roberto's Winds in NYC.[94]

Chapter 4

Elder Statesman (Last Years)

What do they say? "Die with your boots on?" . . . the old gunfighters? Well, I'll die with my reed on, you know. [Laughs]
—Herman "Junior" Cook

Last Years

Cook—the quintessential New York hard bop tenor. Cook—the gentle soul. Cook—leading by example on the jam session stage. Cook—the quiet giant with the one-liners that make you, and him, chuckle. Cook—alone in New York City, deprived of the community that sustained him. These were Junior Cook's last years. But the music. Always, the music.

Outwardly introverted, Cook opened up only among his closest circle of friends. A feature article in the *Sydney Morning Herald* in 1991 described him as "shy," "no celebrity," and "low-key."[1] In the company of the members of the Hardman quintet and their spouses, Cook was talkative, happy. Saxophonist Fred Daniels hosted Cook when the latter commuted from Canada to New York City to play with Freddie Hubbard and remembers Cook having heated yet playful conversations with Daniels's three-year old son over which cartoon to watch: Daniels's son wanted to watch Bugs Bunny, while Cook voted for Mister Magoo. Saxophone repair tech Roberto Romeo recalled Cook playing paper airplanes with Romeo's son at his shop in New York City. Cook's fondness for those closest circles underscored his need for friendship, which in turn may have drawn him into a depression when those circles were broken—for example when Hardman relocated to France and, later, when Hardman died.

Mickey Tucker's memories of Cook's sense of humor made him and his wife both laugh out loud during interviews in early 2022. During the Hardman–Cook quintet's return from a European tour, Tucker remembered a "redneck" on the plane who saw the band and heard them talking. The spectator called out to the musicians, "Y'all boys a band??" Cook replied, without missing a beat, "No! We're all individuals!"[2]

Vibraphonist Don Moors also remarked on Cook's "comic bent, like Dizzy [Gillespie], hilariously funny." He recalled gigging with Cook at Montreal's Black Bottom club in 1968. They arrived at the venue and the sign in the window advertised, "Don Moors Quintet, featuring Junior Cook." Moors recounted, "First thing Junior did was turn to me and say, 'Where's my "feature" money?'" Later, Cook visited the bar to get a drink and returned to the band with a handful of Canadian money, complaining, "This motherfucker just took twenty dollars from me and gave me back monopoly money!" At the hotel Cook was changing clothes when a young lady walked into the room unannounced. She apologized for disturbing them, and Cook later consoled her, "Don't worry about it . . . those tight black pants I was wearing were my legs."[3]

Another anecdote pitted Cook and Shaw in an argument at some point in the early or mid-1980s. Shaw's health began to decline, and he began to lose his eyesight, but not his temper; some speculated that Shaw's declining health and visual incapacity possibly heightened his anger-as-defensiveness. One night Shaw was in the kitchen of the Star Café in New York City attempting to argue with Cook about some matter, but Shaw's failing eyesight led him astray and he couldn't see where Cook was in the room. Cook and a few others in the kitchen let Shaw continue to rant for a while before Cook butted in, "Woody! You're cussing out the refrigerator."[4]

Cook wore, and misplaced, countless pairs of sunglasses—those $2 shades from random vendors crowded around NYC subway exits. Cook used the sunglasses at least in part to compensate for his shyness. The sunglasses hid his eyes and obviated the need to engage, as those nearby could not confirm that Cook saw them or acknowledged their presence. One night Cook had donned a pair of large, dark sunglasses for the gig. Comedian Bill Cosby was in the audience. He later greeted Cook and, thinking him blind because of the glasses, complimented Cook on how well he could get around on the bandstand without assistance.

Cook was about the music. Shepherd said they "never stopped playing," offering a typical schedule:

- Arrive at the Star Café for the gig, 9:00 pm start. Play gig till midnight.
- Cook would then kick off the jam session at the Star Café, midnight till 4:00 am.
- Make their way to the Forty-Third Street residence of a drummer (Hakim) for a jam.
- Get some sleep.
- Play some tunes from 4:00 to 5:00 pm.
- Get something to eat.
- Back to Star Café for the 9:00 pm hit.

Trumpeter Richie Vitale also remembered a hang with Cook, playing at one of several after-hours clubs. "After-hours" in this context meant the early morning hours after the Star Café jam. Cook and Vitale would depart the Star Café at 4:00 am and travel to the after-hours joint, Joyce's on Columbus Circle. Vitale remembered Joyce's as a literal speakeasy, possibly operating illegally, as the city mandated that alcohol could only be served during certain hours. Cook and Vitale would arrive and knock on the door; someone on the inside would open a circular peephole, see Cook at the door (June, they sometimes called him), and let them in. Joyce's bandstand was on a loft, and Vitale, trumpet in one hand, would use the other hand to climb up to the loft to play. Cook and Vitale would play at Joyce's until about 8:00 am, and then Vitale would drive Cook home in his 1973 Plymouth Duster, passing by NYC policemen who, in Cook's words, were "cooping," or catching a nap during those early hours, in their squad cars.

Cook's routine included practice regimens designed to challenge himself. For example, he would practice out of a piano book—not Hanon or another exercise book, according to Shepherd, but Debussy, for example.[5] Cook would play the melodies, transposing from concert to the key for his B-flat tenor saxophone as he read. Saxophonist Ralph Lalama recounted that Cook would call standards in different keys during the Star Café jam or at his own gigs to maintain proficiency in lesser-played keys. For example, Lalama remembered Cook calling the jazz standard "This Song Is You" in G concert and calling a tune based on rhythm changes in the key of B concert, rather than the usual B-flat concert. The phrase "rhythm changes" is shorthand to refer to the chord progressions for George Gershwin's composition, "I Got Rhythm." Composers have used those chord progressions as a basis to compose new jazz melodies, including "Oleo" (Sonny Rollins), "Webb City" (Bud Powell), and "Rhythm-a-Ning" (Thelonius Monk), and "Beltway Rhythm" (Courtney Nero). The technical term for this new melody creation using extant chord progressions is a "contrafact."[6]

"Osmosis"

Cook imparted the wisdom of a seasoned professional on the bandstand in concert and leading NYC jam sessions. Asked plainly "What did you learn from Junior?" pianist Tardo Hammer set the scene succinctly:

> It's amazing you can learn so much and not be told anything. I wonder how it got done. It turns out there's something called nonverbal communication. It's a crucial part of the education that anybody got. I would say the primary mode of education was . . . I guess we would call it "osmosis," the soaking in of feelings and phrasings and modes of doing that happens just from being next to people who do it. Like if you were in the Count Basie band in 1937 and you played every night for several years, you might come off the [tour] bus with a pretty good beat, right? The ability to phrase and just a certain kind of thing that you would take with you from being next to it and wouldn't necessarily require anyone

> to say anything. So that's the primary thing. I don't think I got enough, but I'm grateful for what I got.[7]

Whether he was leading by example or through rare verbal reminders, musicians recalled Cook demonstrating a number of best practices, guiding lights of musicianship and of life. The musicians—Hammer, Shepherd, Su Terry, Vitale, Weiss, and others—carry these principles forward in their own playing, on their own gigs, and in their own instruction to the next generation of jazz musicians.

"No Lulls!"

Cook would push musicians on the bandstand to keep the energy on the stage and to think proactively about set lists, programming, and which songs would comprise a good set. Cook did not like to keep audiences waiting while band members decided on the next tune to play. Pianist Michael Weiss surmised that this may have been a by-product of Horace Silver's influence because Silver ran such a "tight ship."[8] Silver's repertoire, recordings, and concerts were marked by tight arrangements, crisp introductions, shout-chorus interludes, and lively, bouncing sets. Weiss also shared about Cook in an interview for *Cadence* magazine: "[Cook] solidified ideas that I had about various performance practices. Certain aspects of arrangements, like how to start a tune strong and end a tune well. Creating a certain arrangement on a piece instead of just a head-solos-head (approach). How to present a piece with professional decorum."[9]

Participate in the Band Even When not Soloing

Cook remained engaged with the band through the entire song. He generally was not one to play his solo and then leave the bandstand or go to the bar when others were taking their solos. In Cook's view, everyone had a responsibility to make the band better. For example, he would play riffs behind other soloists to push those soloists in their improvisations and to create additional layers and textures within the music. These backgrounds were a Horace Silver staple and, further, a variation on the big band tradition.[10] The riffs kept things interesting for both the listener and the musician and broke the monotony of

Cook's driving background riff underneath Woody Shaw's solo on the "A" section of "Ichi-Ban" (live).

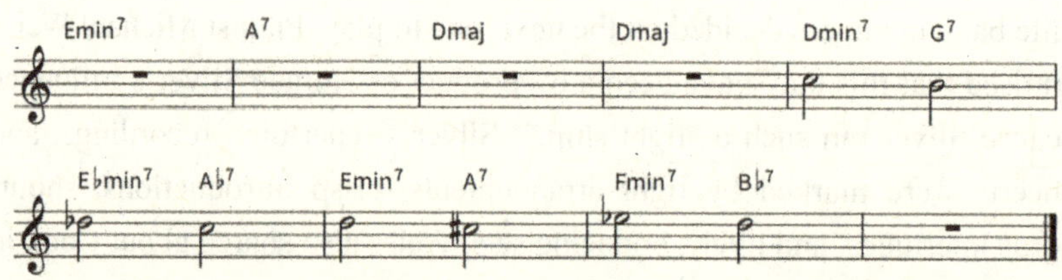

Cook's "B" section backgrounds, outlining the chords (from the flatted seventh degree of one chord to the third degree of the next chord) on "Ichi-Ban" (live).

the solo-after-solo routine, according to Weiss.[11] Cook can be heard on the Ronnie Mathews composition "Ichi-Ban" playing backgrounds behind both Woody Shaw and Ronnie Mathews on their solos during a performance in Germany (*Louis Hayes/Junior Cook Quintet: At Onkel Po's Carnegie Hall, Hamburg 1976*).

Guide Tone Lines

Saxophonist Ralph Moore recalled Cook's devotion to harmony in his attention to guide tone lines—pitches that connect each chord in a chord progression. Guide tone pitches can construct a pathway to move through a set of chord changes. In so doing the guide tone lines provide the musician a melodic reference for approaching an improvised solo over the tune. (Others refer to voice leading, a similar-sounding concept that often implies movement between chords using the smallest musical interval possible. It's conceivable that Cook's guide tone lines referred to the same process that others called voice leading.) Cook believed in guide tone lines as a roadmap to harmony, according to Moore. At the Star Café jam session, if Moore missed chords on a tune, Cook would take Moore to the kitchen of the Star Café, play through the guide tone lines on his horn, and then send Moore out to return to the stage and solo again. Moore recalled that his return to the stage for a second solo—when there were lines of horn players waiting to play—sometimes drew the ire of the waiting session participants, but Cook was Moore's cover: "Junior told me to come back out."[12]

Moore jotted down guide tone lines for the tune "High Fly" to demonstrate one way that Cook might approach it. Inasmuch as the tune "High Fly" is composed mostly of ii-V (two-five) progressions, many of the guide tones move from the flatted-seventh degree of the ii chord to the third degree of the V chord; the distance between those two pitches is a semitone, or half step. For example, in the first two measures, the guide tone D-natural (flatted-seventh degree of the E-minor^{7}) leads to the next guide tone, C-sharp (third degree of the A-dominant^{7} chord).

Maintain the Variety

Cook demanded diversity in the repertoire on the bandstand and challenged his fellow musicians to stretch themselves with respect to programming. To keep the repertoire interesting, "Once we play [a tune based on] rhythm changes, that's it," he was remembered to say. Vocalist Shepherd, for example, might sing an Eddie Jefferson tune on a gig; if he tried to call another one, Cook would interject, "You did one of those already," pushing Shepherd to broaden his repertoire. Trumpeter Richie Vitale remembered that the variety served at least two purposes: it reflected both how mindful Cook was to give his audience a good show and his relentless desire to improve his craft.[13] Cook never felt like he had mastered the horn. He was always reaching in his practice habits, in his improvisations, and in his repertoire. Weiss recalled in an interview that

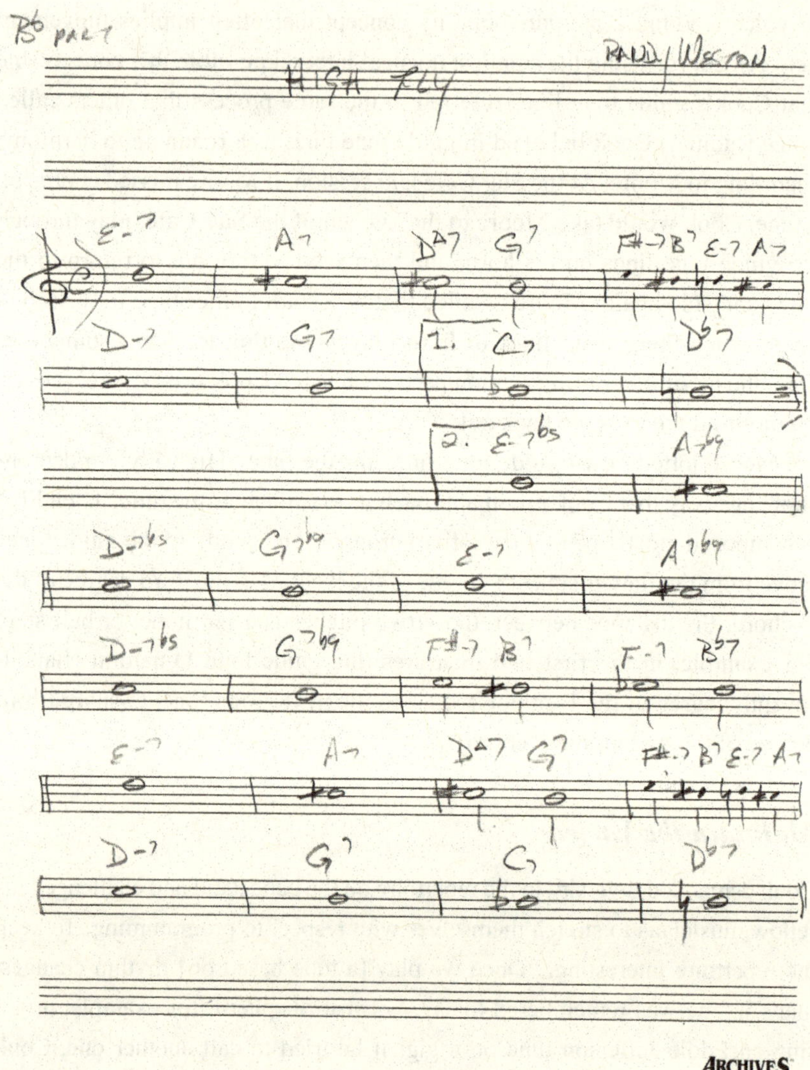

Approach to guide tone lines on Randy Weston's "High Fly," written for Bb instruments Courtesy of Ralph Moore.

Cook "was always interested in playing different repertoires, out of the ordinary compositions by Monk, Gigi Gryce, Kenny Dorham, rare standards that haven't been done to death, things like that."[14] Weiss also shared in an online forum the variety of tunes that he would play with Cook:

> Monk [Thelonius Monk]: Round Midnight, Gallop's Gallop, Off Minor, Brake's Sake, Eronel, Well You Needn't
>
> Trane [John Coltrane]: Lazy Bird, Moment's Notice, Take the Coltrane, Crescent, Naima
>
> Standards Trane recorded: You Leave Me Breathless, If There is Someone Lovelier Than You, I'm a Dreamer Aren't We All, You Say You Care, Rise and Shine, The Night Has a Thousand Eyes, Time Was
>
> Other standards: It Could Happen to You, Bye Bye Blackbird, By Myself, Like Someone in Love, When Sunny Gets Blue, Girl Talk, Old Folks, Moment to Moment, Detour Ahead, End of a Love Affair, Make the Man Love Me (Dinah Washington), Once I Loved, Over the Rainbow, Wave, What's New, Without a Song
>
> Tadd [Dameron]: Mating Call, Gnid, On a Misty Night
>
> KD [Kenny Dorham]: La Mesha, Una Mas
>
> Donald Byrd: Fly Little Bird Fly
>
> Bird [Charlie Parker]: She Rote
>
> J. J. [Johnson]: Enigma (from BN Miles)
>
> Cedar [Walton]: Firm Roots
>
> We used to play Conception as a hybrid of Miles' and Bud's arrangements.[15]

Play the "Present"

Drummer Joe Farnsworth relayed that Cook would refuse requests to play those Horace Silver compositions that Cook himself had helped become standards in the jazz canon. Musicians would want to play Silver's "Strollin'," for example, and Cook would blow it off: "That was the '50s. I play 'now.'" The sentiment spoke to Cook's desire to move forward in the music and tracked closely with the elder and younger Shepherds' accounts of Cook's practice regimen, including his attention to harmonic development at the piano and his use of classical piano music for new harmonic forms and to develop and advance his technique on the horn.

Pianist Tardo Hammer recalled greeting Cook at the Star Café or at another gig—"What's happening?"—and Cook's stock response was, "We. Are. Here." Reliving the moment, the depth of the answer weighed on Hammer: "'We. Are. Here.' That doesn't sound like it means much, but it means a lot. Get the other stuff out of your head." We are in *this* moment, at *this* gig, about to play *this* music, on *this* day. Let's get to it. Let's make it happen.[16]

Know Your Harmony

Hazeltine, Shepherd, and saxophonist Su Terry recalled watching Cook play piano before gigs, on breaks, or at home. Hazeltine, as a pianist, said, "I know that he understood harmony very well just by the way he played the piano and that he understood the harmonies of the songs and standards that we played . . . he was very good at that."[17] Pianist Tardo Hammer remembered Cook—and other musicians, including Tommy Turrentine and Clifford Jordan—sitting down to the piano. They wouldn't bang out running torrents of sixteenth notes, but they played chords "with clarity, conviction, and power," according to Hammer, very ably comping for one horn player after another on the jam session bandstand.[18]

Cook had befriended John Coltrane, and personal and press accounts note that Cook shedded with Coltrane, playing chords on the piano as Coltrane worked out what would become his original composition "Giant Steps."[19]

Embrace the "Pulse" of the Music

Saxophonist Su Terry recalled being entranced at Cook's ability to play at so-called flag tempos, slang for fast music, so effortlessly. She observed that Cook would pat his foot only on the first beat of a measure, rather than on two and four, which is often counseled in jazz pedagogy. In this Terry gathered that Cook had internalized his sense of time, "feeling the pulse" and "riding the pulse" of the tempo. Terry mimicked the approach, and it improved her own sense of time and mastery of faster tempos.[20]

The Stage is Sacred

This mantra is not unique to Cook; Silver, Blakey, and many other bandleaders proclaimed the same. Farnsworth remembered that the band area in

Augie's was not a stage or bandstand in the literal sense of the word. Rather than being a raised platform, the stage was floor level. Musicians and patrons alike had to walk past it to get to the bathrooms in the back of the club. Nonetheless, in Cook's mind he drew an imaginary line that delineated that sacred space; when you crossed that line, it was imperative to respect the space, whether the performance was a $50 gig or Carnegie Hall. Cook's respect for the stage demanded that he gave the music his all; Farnsworth and others recounted that you would never have known Cook's health challenges by his on-stage performance.[21]

Pace Yourself

Cook counseled Farnsworth to play a two-four feel on the first two choruses of each horn player's solo at the Augie's jams. With four or five or six horn players waiting in the wings, that would be a lot of two-four. Farnsworth appreciated, however, that it taught him to pace himself, acknowledging that arranging and pacing were two traits that Cook likely learned early on from being in Silver's quintet. On a gig at the Flamingo Lounge in Brooklyn, Farnsworth asked Cook for advice to improve, and just at that moment the club's jukebox started to play Miles Davis's "Walkin'," with J. J. Johnson on trombone and Kenny Clarke on drums. In Kenny Clarke Farnsworth heard a patient presence and rock-solid time. Clarke was listening and interacting, contributing as a member of the unit, not as an individual. Cook said, "Listen to Kenny Clarke . . . playing the cymbal like that. That's all I want. That's all anybody wants."[22]

Make Your Statement

Trumpeter Richie Vitale recalled Cook often saying of young musicians taking the bandstand during a jam, "If you can't say it in two or three choruses, you can't say it." Vitale said that young tenor saxophone players were often the "worst offenders," playing chorus after chorus on a jam session song, even though there were maybe a dozen other horn players waiting their turns in the wings. Weary of long-winded horn players, Cook and Vitale sometimes would start playing backgrounds while the horn player was soloing to encourage a conclusion. If the horn player didn't take the hint, they would play backgrounds again on the next chorus, or just start spontaneously clapping for the horn player.[23]

Just Play

Farnsworth, Michael Weiss, and Bill Pierce remembered that Cook for the most part was not one to counsel musicians at the "Play this, don't play that" level. Cook's advice: "Just play," "Keep doing what you're doing." Development comes with time on target. "Just play" nods to the need to be in the music to move forward in it.[24]

Be a "Heavyweight"

Su Terry sat in with the Hardman–Cook quintet for a performance at the Lincoln Center. Cook invited her to sit in. (Terry always carried her saxophone, ready to sit in, but she never asked; she waited to be invited.) The group played the standard "Stella by Starlight." Terry admitted knowing parts of the song better than others. After the performance Cook counseled her, drawing on his love of boxing for an analogy: "If you're going to go in the ring with a heavyweight, you better be a heavyweight." Terry elaborated on what Cook's words meant to her: "So, number one: if you are not of an equal 'weight class,' i.e., caliber, then you should not engage with the person, at least not on stage. But also, you have to have an 'inner feeling' of being at the caliber, or at least aspiring to that caliber. This inner feeling cannot be a pretend feeling. It has to be authentic, based on doing the daily work and the constant contemplation and focus in one's area of study."[25]

*****

Cook transferred his professorial chair in the late 1980s from the Star Café to Augie's jazz club, where he continued to invest in younger musicians by example, if not with explicit instruction. Joe Farnsworth met Cook circa 1989, when pianist Tardo Hammer invited Farnsworth to a jam session at Bill Hardman's Brooklyn home. Farnsworth met Hardman and Cook at that jam; Hardman's and Cook's reputations preceded them based on their individual accomplishments and the notoriety of the Hardman–Cook quintet.

When Farnsworth was tapped to run the jam session at Augie's jazz club, he imagined what a coup it would be to get Cook to come to the jam. Farnsworth was reluctant to call him, but Hardman encouraged him to ask. Farnsworth decided to approach Cook about the Augie's hit at Sweet Basil's jazz club, where Nat Adderley was performing with Cook as a special guest. "Cook was kicking ass," Farnsworth recalled. Noncommittal in the moment, two weeks later Cook came to the Augie's jam, played "Sweet Pumpkin," and left the club. He later connected with Farnsworth and committed to attend.[26]

Cook never made the first set of the three-set-night. Farnsworth characterized that the first set was comparatively tame, and after the first set, "It was Junior time." Cook would enter the club like Wyatt Earp, coming through the doors with his tenor, an alto, sometimes a flute, and sometimes a baritone saxophone. "Call the fire marshal!" he'd often proclaim, remarking on the number of musicians waiting on the sidelines to play. He playfully called Farnsworth the "white Buhaina," referring to Art Blakey's adopted Muslim name, and would try to ease what he described as Farnsworth's edgy, rushing, "white nervousness." Cook also needled neophyte musicians at the Augie's jam with another joke from his comedic repertoire: "We're gonna play 'Half Nelson,'" a bebop standard composed by Miles Davis. Cook continued with the punchline, "I know [the song] 'Full Nelson' but y'all aren't ready for it."[27]

Cook's playing was relaxed intensity, Farnsworth recalled. He was laid back, but with a fire. Big, fat, long tones and beautiful melodies. "Trane changes but his own shit." Cook would play into a mic connected to the guitar player's amp and go to town. Farnsworth declared the years 1989, 1990, and 1991 as "the best times ever" with Cook, who was a "superstar" to him and to the Augie's jam regulars. There was a special respect and esteem among many of the younger musicians for Cook.[28]

Cook was known and loved by musicians and those who knew him, while the jazz music industry, searching for the next young star, plodded along without much thought for him. Cook's laid-back approach to pushing his name and his craft did him no favors in an industry always on the lookout for the "flavor of the month," as he put it in a 1991 press interview.[29] Saxophonist Kelly Shepherd remembered Cook's sense of resignation to his status in the industry in a postgig conversation. The young Shepherd, in his late teens circa 1987, traveled to an inn outside Philadelphia to hear Cook in concert, possibly the Deer Head Inn in Delaware Water Gap, Pennsylvania, or one of a few other Poconos jazz venues. Saxophonist Arnie Lawrence and pianist-composer-arranger-vocalist Bob Dorough attended as well to hear Cook, whom Lawrence during the night called "the greatest living tenor saxophone player."[30] (Cook and altoist Lawrence switched horns at one point in the night and played "Cherokee," Cook on alto and Lawrence on tenor.) After the gig Shepherd joined Cook in his room. The inn treated Cook to a feast—one of those meals on a rolling tray with a big silver dome on top, according to Shepherd. As Shepherd prepared to depart for the night, he said to Cook, "Thanks for the music. Is there anybody writing a book about you??" Cook responded, "I know you mean well. I can't get a gig in my hometown [New York City]. They don't want the truth. They want Mike Brecker."[31]

Brecker, a white tenor saxophonist, front lined the Horace Silver quintet with his brother, Randy Brecker, on trumpet in the early 1970s and was a fixture in New York City studios and in live performances. The timing of Cook's passing comment about Michael Brecker may have coincided with the release of Brecker's self-titled debut album as a leader on the Impulse! label in 1987, an event that more than likely garnered lots of marketing, media attention, and genuine excitement about this milestone in Brecker's career.

Undoubtedly talented, innovative, and a virtuoso of the instrument, Brecker all the same was frequently a foil among some Black musicians, who perceived media and marketing attention invested in him while Black musicians—veteran jazz artists as well as younger, Brecker peers—received comparatively less notice. Brecker similarly was the target of criticism from Joe Henderson, who claimed in a 1992 *DownBeat* interview that Brecker "stole his shit" and had failed to rightfully acknowledge his (Henderson's) influence on Brecker's playing.[32] Whether Henderson's charges were merited or not—according to Bill Milkowski's book *Ode to a Tenor Titan*, Henderson (dubiously) made the same claims of John Coltrane—Henderson's allegations illustrated some Black musicians' simmering resentment and perception of white musicians as interlopers in jazz, which was born uniquely out of the Black American experience.[33]

Tenorist Ralph Moore remembered a similar quip from Cook in the late 1980s. Moore and Cook had crossed paths at Roberto's Winds, and conversation turned toward one of Moore's early recording releases as a leader, which was starting to get some airplay. Cook warned Moore that day, "Don't worry . . . they will forget you as fast as they discovered you." Moore did not take it as a put-down but rather as an education: "Don't let it go to your head." Moore, however, also read in Cook's offering a certain measure of cynicism, though not directed toward him personally. Moore observed that the older cats, "the heart and soul of the music," were often overlooked, written out, and passed over, and "lived hand to mouth the whole way." There was "no safety net for those guys," no safety net "for *that* part of New York."[34]

Ralph Moore, for his part, lamented "how New York treated" Junior Cook and many other players of that era, nodding to the tough lifestyle that they often lived for the music. Moore said it was "brutally competitive" back in those days and held out as an example his 1980s gigs at Dude's Lounge, which paid about $50 for five sets of music, or the Star Café, which paid between $15 and $25. Moore also alluded to some racial divides that persisted in the music, recalling that many white musicians would gravitate toward some of the lingering big bands of the day: Woody Herman, Maynard Ferguson, Buddy Rich, Doc Severinsen. By contrast, what Moore described as the "hardcore, uptown jazz scene" was predominantly Black and often less well paid.[35]

On Cook's last leader recordings on the SteepleChase label from 1988 to 1991, one can still hear the unique musical voice that kept Cook working consistently among ensembles. His sound, in comparison with the Hubbard/Hayes/Hardman years, perhaps had downshifted by one gear: Back to his flowing, melodic eighth notes, Cook seemed to have pulled back from his approach that Slide Hampton once mentioned was "approaching the energy comparable to Trane and Sonny."[36] His attack, still timely, seemed a tad less sharp. One could divine a certain sonic patina on his tone: maybe less air in the horn, maybe a millisecond longer to translate right-brain creativity to his fingers.

Cook recorded *The Place to Be* for SteepleChase in 1988, a release in which he showed "himself as potent as ever," according to an *Los Angeles Times* review that gave the album "four stars." The review described Cook's "driving, resplendent lines" on up-tempo tracks, like Charlie Parker's "She Rote," and his "singing, provocative statements" on Tucker's ballad "I Should Have Known."[37] Tim Smith's review for *Cadence* magazine noted that Cook was "his usual dependable self" on the recording, which showcased his "tough but warm tone" in a "Blue Note-ish recording that sounds remarkably fresh, especially when compared to much of the neo-bop currently being recorded."[38]

Cook followed that project with another for SteepleChase, *On a Misty Night*, in 1989, an apparent homage to the compositional prowess of composer Tadd Dameron and again tipping his hat to John Coltrane, who recorded the same tune on 1950s album releases. Cook's performance is light, fluid, almost carefree, nothing to prove and everything to gain in presenting the sum total of his musical self. He seemingly can't resist quoting "Just Squeeze Me" in the second chorus of the title track before handing the tune to bass player Walter Booker for a solo, supported by the effortless interplay of Mickey Tucker on piano and Leroy Williams on drums. The album otherwise is Cook being Cook, reveling in songs that he loved and the composers that he esteemed. The project included Mickey Tucker's composition "Innocent One"; "Wabash," a Sunny-Side-of-the-Street Sunday stroll of a composition by his fellow Floridian Cannonball Adderley, complete with a well-timed "Nostalgia" half quote; "You Know Who" by Bertha Hope; American songbook tunes "Make the Girl Love Me" (Schwartz and Fields), "Nothing Ever Changes" (Segal and Fisher), and "I'll Go My Way by Myself" (Schwartz and Dietz); and one of his favorites, "My Sweet Pumpkin," which he played at his Augie's debut with Joe Farnsworth.

Cook in fact had a veritable run on the SteepleChase label, both with his own recordings and as sideman on others' projects, including Bill Hardman's *What's Up* (1989, Hardman's last album), Bertha Hope's *Elmo's Fire* (1991), and Louis Smith's *Strike Up the Band* (1991).

Cook's health began to decline noticeably in the last few years of his life, possibly as early as the mid-1980s. Saxophone repair tech Roberto Romeo recalled Cook visiting the shop and presenting a very frail and tired figure, sometimes sleeping in the chair in the shop. Roberto would repair and maintain Cook's horn free of charge, and they bonded in friendship. As Cook's health declined, musicians called on Roberto to try to convince Cook to see a doctor, but with little apparent success.[39]

Cook's habits did him no favors. One night at the club, Cook ordered a vodka but the bartender delivered gin instead. Cook highlighted the error to the bartender, who then corrected the mistake by providing Cook a glass of vodka. The error and the order both before him, Cook poured the gin and the vodka into one glass and downed the concoction. Drummer Joe Farnsworth, who was with Cook and witnessed the incident, wondered what the concocktail would do to Cook's insides. Substance abuse in various forms may have been Cook's way of dealing with the jazz musician's life in that era. It may have been a means to stave off depression, though Shepherd believes it likely contributed to Cook's depression.

Cook visited Roberto's Winds in 1990 after hearing of Bill Hardman's death. After hanging out for a bit, Cook asked to use the bathroom, which was accessed by walking through Roberto's shop. Cook spent a while in the bathroom, ten minutes or more by Roberto's recollection, but raising only mild suspicion. Cook eventually emerged—"See you, man"—and left the store. Roberto checked out the bathroom later and spied two empty vodka bottles, likely from Cook self-medicating to cope with Hardman's death.[40]

Tardo Hammer recalled a conversation with bassist Jamil Nasser about how out of it Cook appeared following Hardman's death. According to Hammer, whatever health ailments Cook nursed, he was a "powerhouse" on stage with the horn in his hand until Hardman passed. To Hammer, Cook was gray and became weak, a shadow of himself. Nasser offered that Cook eventually died "of a broken heart," alluding again to Cook's close relationship with Hardman. Though a romantic connotation is often affixed to that phrase, Hammer honed in specifically on the heart as the seat of motivation, inspiration, and courage. Nasser proffered, in that sense, that Hardman's death sapped many of those traits from Cook—his motivation, his drive, his inspiration, and his courage.[41]

Advertisement for Michael Weiss trio featuring Junior Cook at Scullers Jazz Club, Boston, Massachusetts, 20 October 1991. *Boston Globe*, October 20, 1991, p. 98.

Cook visited the Tuckers in Australia in early to mid-October 1991. Cook and Tucker reunited and played gigs there. Cook sat in with Tucker's jazz trio at Doctor Jazz, a club in Melbourne. Press recaps described Cook's playing as "displaying a full, attractive tenor tone and constructing logical, flowing solos." Journalist Adrian Jackson described Cook's music as "full of conviction" and called the night "exhilarating."[42] Those adjectives, however, did not carry over to Cook's constitution. Cook's musical health seemed to contrast with his physical well-being. By Tucker's account Cook appeared very feeble and just didn't look like himself. Tucker remembered telling his wife, Sheila, that he didn't think he would see Cook alive again.[43]

Back in the States, pianist Michael Weiss secured Cook's participation for a performance at Scullers jazz club (Boston) in late October 1991, rounding out the Michael Weiss Quartet, which also featured Tony Scherr on bass and Andy Watson on drums. Weiss recalled that Cook was out of sorts—"testy, cranky," and "in a foul mood"—on the three-plus-hour drive from New York City to Boston. Perhaps Cook's declining health made the trip more difficult.

Perhaps the drive was too long a trip without a drink. Perhaps Cook was still feeling the aftereffects of round-trip air travel to Australia. Perhaps it was all of the above. Weiss chose to keep his distance, as much as one can in the same car.[44]

*****

Weiss's Scullers set list featured many of the tunes in Cook's concert repertoire of the day. National Public Radio's radio program *JazzSet* broadcast excerpts of the Scullers concert:

1st Set

"The End of a Love Affair"
"Off Minor"
"Somewhere Over the Rainbow"
"Budini" (trio) a Buddy Montgomery composition
"Gnid"
"Lazy Bird"
"The Theme"
"Once I Loved"

2nd Set

"On a Misty Night"
"By Myself"
"Make the Man Love Me"
"I'll Remember April" (trio)
"Eronel"
"Take the Coltrane"
"The Theme"

Cook's playing was a masterclass in improvisational pacing, melodic sensitivity, and voice leading. The treatment of the classic ballad "Somewhere Over the Rainbow," from the movie *The Wizard of Oz*, let the listener know that the song is not in Kansas anymore. Weiss recalled that the arrangement may have originated with Cedar Walton. Cook weaved through the changes with ease and lyricism, including tritone substitutions very familiar to him and present in his treatment of other jazz standards, including "All the Things You Are" and "Confirmation."

The advertisement for the Scullers gig (see p. 92)—"Michael Weiss Trio featuring Junior Cook"—testified to Cook's ability to build and maintain a vast network of musicians to nurture steady work. Tardo Hammer relayed an instance where he was trying to help Cook with marketing and was gently rebuked for the effort. Hammer took the initiative to print some business cards for Cook's use; "Junior Cook Quartet" was written on the cards. Cook took one look at the business cards and said to Hammer, "You trying to get me in trouble, man?" By Hammer's account Cook was reluctant (at least in this instance) to promote or advertise that he was leading a quartet with specific rhythm section personnel, lest other musicians stop calling him, thinking that he was tied down with one band. Hammer realized Cook's stance, and said out loud, "Oh. It should say the 'Tardo Hammer Quartet, featuring Junior Cook.'" Cook responded, "Thank you." In some cases Cook preferred to advertise gigs as a performing unit—Michael Weiss trio, Tardo Hammer quartet—"featuring Junior Cook" as a signal that he was always on the market for work. He had as many dance cards to hand out as musicians who wanted to dance. It apparently worked. As Hammer recalled, if you went out and knew where to go, "You could catch Junior several nights a week playing somewhere," either on a jam or as the feature tenor with an ensemble.[45]

Hammer recalled playing a trio gig featuring Cook at a club called Paris "in the valley" on Broadway. They played the gig for about six months.

> You know we had a gig up here . . . so I'm on the hill, on the west side of upper Manhattan, and Junior was on the hill on the east side of upper Manhattan. And one day—I guess it was around 1989, I think, or '90, probably '90—I was walking by a place and there was an upright piano. This was in the valley. Broadway, in between these two hills. I went in. It was the only time I ever cold-sold a gig and the next thing we had every Thursday night. It was Junior and . . . usually if they could make it, it was Leroy [Williams] and Dennis Irwin. And we'd play every Thursday. It paid decently considering it was 1990 and things don't pay much more than that now. And it was a pretty good night.[46]

Hammer reminisced that Cook would travel to the gig on foot through New York City's well-known St. Nicholas Tunnel, to which Hammer referred once as the "JC Tunnel" in honor of Cook:

> You know I'm going off topic. . . . There's a tunnel here for the subway, the one train that comes from . . . it's like several blocks long. It's really funky. There's graffiti and garbage in there and stuff. And if you lived up on the hill where Junior lived, you would take the elevator down to go to this gig that was on Broadway. And after the first set [at this gig at Paris on Broadway], I might go and look up the tunnel and see if Junior was gonna show up for the gig because he would . . . you could see him walking all the way down at the end of the tunnel. And he'd have his horn and his sunglasses, his cap on. "Oh, here comes Junior Cook." And it's a long, straight tunnel. And it emerges on Broadway, and you come out and then next door, maybe three doors up was this pub we were playing at. And it's a legendary tunnel because nobody wants to walk through it, 'cause it's funky. And my goal is that I want it named after Junior and have some stuff in there, maybe some sounds and pictures in the tunnel. It'll never happen, but maybe if your book comes out. . . . It's 191st Street, one train stop. It's at St. Nicholas Avenue but if you have to get out to Broadway . . . I guess it's two long avenue blocks from St. Nicholas Avenue to Broadway, underground. It emerges right at street level at Broadway. Pedestrian tunnel to get into the subway. I used to watch every Thursday to see if Junior would show up for the gig. I'd watch, walk up and look down that tunnel on the break and eventually he would turn up. I want it named after him.[47]

If Cook's approach to networking and gigging amounted to a sideman's life, it also afforded him the "no strings" flexibility to flow among various recording labels. Many record labels are represented in Cook's discography: Blue Note, Prestige, Riverside, Epic, Xanadu, and SteepleChase.

Cook in late 1991 asked Farnsworth to participate in what would be Cook's last recording. Cook called Farnsworth in the morning at the latter's girlfriend's house—Farnsworth to this day doesn't know how Cook got the number—to ask if he was available for the recording session since drummer Leroy Williams was out of town. The session, Cook's *You Leave Me Breathless* on the SteepleChase label, was Farnsworth's recording debut. Mickey Tucker (piano), John Webber (bass), and Valery Ponomarev (trumpet) also were in the band for the session. The set featured two Ponomarev compositions ("Junior's Cook" ["One for Morgans"] and "Envoy"); Duke Ellington's "Warm Valley"; Tucker's "Sweet Lotus Lips"; Miles Davis's "Vierd Blues"; the title track "You Leave Me Breathless" by Frederick Hollander; Cedar Walton's "Fiesta Español," which Cook had recorded before; and Coltrane's "Mr. P. C." In an article shortly after Cook's death, Steve Voce, writing for *The Independent* (UK), minced no words in contrasting Cook's deteriorating health and the music of the *You Leave Me Breathless* recording session. He wrote, "Although his [Cook's] appearance was awful, his playing retained all its old fire."[48]

Tucker and Cook reunited yet once more, but this time Cook's health got the best of their effort to make music together again. Tucker returned to the States in late 1991 to record for SteepleChase in New York City. SteepleChase founder Nils Winther made periodic trips from Copenhagen to New York City for recording dates. Tenor saxophonist and Jazz Messengers alumnus Javon Jackson remembered those sessions as very efficient, if not harried. Winther scheduled consecutive, multihour blocks over the course of a day to fit in multiple group sessions; he shared via an email interview that SteepleChase needed "to run a tight ship."[49]

Tucker had planned to feature Cook on tenor, but Cook's declining, frail condition dictated otherwise. The day before the session, Cook called Freddie Hubbard to get in touch with young tenorist Javon Jackson. Jackson had started his first week playing in Hubbard's quintet in late 1991. On a gig at Fat Tuesdays in NYC, Hubbard told Jackson that Cook wanted to talk to him. In the ensuing phone conversation, Cook said that he needed Jackson on standby for Tucker's SteepleChase session the next day. Cook reportedly was under the weather and unsure he would make the date. The day of the session, Jackson arrived at the studio near Eighth Avenue and Tucker showed him the music. Cook was not present at the start of the session. When Cook did arrive at the studio, he was clearly weak. Jackson recalled Cook lying on the studio floor for most of the session.[50] Winther relied on his session notes and memory to recount that Cook played on the session, but none of his tenor takes appeared on the released album.[51]

Winther remembered that Cook was sick and very weak on that date, so much so that Jackson covered the tenor duties for the 9 December 1991 recording session. The recorded tracks would be released on SteepleChase as Tucker's leader date, entitled *Hang in There*. Cook's condition struck Winther, who did not remember Cook being so frail less than a week earlier at Cook's own recording session, for the album *You Leave Me Breathless*, recorded 6 December 1991.

Available pictures (some included here) illustrate the change in Cook's appearance from about the mid-1980s. He seemed to have aged rapidly, losing some weight and appearing gaunt in the face. Having sported a neat Afro for most of his life with a Fu Manchu mustache and beard, his trademark in the late 1980s and early 1990s included a kufi-type skull cap. A drawing of Cook and Michael Weiss, dated circa 1984, pictured the Afro'ed Cook. Just a few years later, pictures of the Hardman–Cook quintet in Paris, at a gathering at the Tucker home (1986), and on the cover of his *On a Misty Night* album portrayed his declining health. His head bald and covered, his skin weathered and clean-shaven, Cook took the form of a man some twenty years his senior. Vibraphonist Don Moors on his website described Cook playfully as "doing his famous Elijah Muhammad impression" aside the photo featured on the cover of Cook's *You Leave Me Breathless* album, using the religious leader as reference for Cook's gaunt appearance and head covering.[52] (Muhammad died at age 77, while Cook, who one may argue looked as old as Muhammad, died at 57.) Speaking of doppelgangers, Timmy Shepherd also recalled a beach photo of Cook crowded with random passers-by who had mistaken his tall, dark, and Afro'ed frame for actor Sidney Poitier.[53] Weiss recalled observing Cook in the early 1990s lose his hair over a very short period of time, possibly early indicators of the liver disease and cirrhosis that would claim his life.[54]

Cook played at Augie's the night before he died. The last song of the night was "Jeannine," and Cook played the song that night on alto saxophone. Farnsworth remembered Cook saying, "I started on alto, I'll end on alto." The poignance of that seemingly offhand remark weighed on Farnsworth during his interview for this project some thirty years later, apparently replaying the connection in his head that the tune ended the jam for the night and may have been the last tune Cook ever played. Farnsworth drove Cook home after the gig.[55]

Cook's no-show for an early February 1992 gig was uncharacteristic for him; he would usually emerge just in the nick of time or maybe one set late, but a complete absence was rare. Musicians from uptown and Clifford Jordan both called Roberto's shop, inquiring whether Roberto had put eyes on Cook. (Cook was borrowing a tenor saxophone that belonged to Jordan, a Selmer Mark VI tenor in the 80,000 serial number range. Jordan reportedly was genuinely concerned about Cook but also about the Mark VI horn.) When the doorman at Cook's apartment called Roberto with the same query, it brought an additional urgency to the situation. The doorman was reluctant to force his way into Cook's apartment, out of concern of upsetting Cook if everything was somehow all right. Roberto counseled the doorman to break the lock on Cook's apartment door, assuring him that he (Roberto) would take the heat and pay to replace the lock if necessary.[56]

Cook was found dead in his unit. Initial press reports relayed that he died of undetermined causes, but later coverage reported that he died of cirrhosis. While press accounts differed in their reporting of the date of his death, it is likely that Cook died of cirrhosis on 2 February 1992 and was found in his apartment on 3 February 1992.[57]

Cook's wake was held at John Joyce Funeral Home, New York City, on 9 February 1992, and a funeral mass took place on 10 February 1992. Cook was buried at Restland Cemetery in East Hanover, New Jersey; his brother Robert F. Cook took care of the burial arrangements.[58] The service in Cook's honor was a small one. Louis Hayes, Barry Harris, Leroy Williams, and Cecil Payne attended. Members of Cook's Pensacola family attended as well. His brother Robert and his wife, Eula, traveled to New York to attend the service, and Robert ferried Cook's instruments and possessions back to Florida afterward, according to the recollections of Cook's family.[59] Cook's Boston companion Patricia Landry retained a copy of the funeral program with written notes, indicating that Rudy Van Gelder recited a "prayer of comfort"; vocalist Evelyn Blakey, eldest child of drummer Art Blakey, performed an unspecified selection; and a Reverend Gensel, likely John Garcia Gensel, "minister to the jazz community," provided the eulogy.[60] Drummer Joe Farnsworth carried some heartache for Cook and his isolation in life. He recalled that musicians lamented Cook's death at the time—"Oh, we miss Junior"—but few connected with him or sought his guidance and the musical wisdom that he yearned to share with the younger generation while he lived.[61]

View of 400 block of East Brainerd Street, Pensacola, Florida, July 2023. Photo by the author.

Pensacola, Florida, marker noting Eastside neighborhood (corner of East Cervantes Street and North Davis Highway), July 2023. Photo by the author.

Washington Junior College

WISDOM ★ JUDGMENT ★ COURAGE

BULLETIN 1956-1957

Washington Junior College Bulletin, 1956–1957.
Courtesy of Pensacola State College.

COMPLETE ENROLLMENT DURING 1955-1956

FRESHMEN—WOMEN

1. Baker, Sallie
2. Braziel, Ollie
3. Brooks, Lillian
4. Brown, Dorothy
5. Burton, Eula
6. Calloway, Dora
7. Carter, Gussie
8. Clark, Betty Ann
9. Daniels, Eula
10. Donald, Cassie
11. Donald, Betty
12. Forney, Lula
13. Foster, Annie G.
14. Galry, Lucile
15. Gibson, Viola
16. Gillis, Betty
17. Gooden, Janet
18. Green, Dorothy
19. Hall, Cassie B.
20. Harris, Callie
21. Hicks, Juanita J.
22. Houston, Frenchie
23. Howard, Arlene
24. Howard, Mary
25. Hunter, Clair
26. Inman, Nora
27. Ivy, Rosa
28. Jackson, Mary
29. Johnson, Cynthia
30. Jones, Vastie
31. Lusane, Alma
32. McCullough, Mamie R.
33. Milton, Catherine
34. Moore, Mercy Ella
35. Nelson, Alice
36. Palmer, Elizabeth
37. Price, Dollie
38. Robinson, Helen
39. Rogers, Virginia
40. Ross, Mable
41. Rostchild, Gladys
42. Simmons, Shirley
43. Singer, Catha
44. Smith, Gladys
45. Soles, Bettye
46. Soto, Stella
47. Tripp, Margaret
48. Williams, Sarah
49. Woods, Willie

FRESHMEN—MEN

1. Alexander, Thomas
2. Baldwin, John
3. Booker, William
4. Broughton, Austin
5. Byrd, Willie
6. Cook, Herman
7. Cromartie, Terry J.
8. Crowe, Climmie
9. Crumpton, Tommie
10. Davis, Ezel
11. Duckworth, Robert
12. Epps, Willie D.
13. Ford, Jesse
14. Fountain, Jesse
15. Gainey, Ernest
16. Gray, Raymond
17. Goldsmith, Willie
18. Goodson, Danny
19. Hayes, Rozel
20. Holmes, Eddie
21. Howell, Sidney
22. Hurry, Clifton
23. Jerkins, Jerry
24. Knight, Charlie
25. Lamons, Albert
26. Lee, Johnny
27. Lett, Harold
28. McDuffie, Eston
29. McWilliams, Grover C.
30. Moore, Allen
31. Moore, Harold E.
32. Moorer, Frederick
33. Roberts, Johnny
34. Sampson, Fred
35. Soles, John
36. Todd, Eddie S.
37. Wallace, Alvin
38. Washington, Edward
39. Washington, James
40. Watts, Charles
41. Williams, Reuben
42. Williams, Willie
43. Wynder, Bertram
44. Wynn, Jerry

Washington Junior College enrollment list, 1955–1956.
Courtesy of Pensacola State College.

Robert Cook Sr., brother of Herman Cook. Undated photo, likely in Pensacola, Florida. Courtesy of Angela Harris.

Cook, Herman

WASHINGTON JUNIOR COLLAGE
FINAL RECORD
YEARS

FRESHMAN YEAR

FIRST SEMESTER 1955-56 COURSE	GR	HR	PT	YR	SECOND SEMESTER 1955-56 COURSE	GR	HR	PT	YR
Physical Education	A	1	4	1956	102 Physical Education	A	1	4	
Freshman Communications	A	3	12	"	102 Public School Music	A	3	12	
American History	B	3	9	"	202 Biological Science	B	4	12	
Biological Science	C	4	8	"	102 Fresh. Communications	C	3	6	
Introduction to Mathematics	C	3	6	"	102 Intro. To Mathematics	C	3	6	
Public School Music	A	3	12	"					

SOPHOMORE YEAR

FIRST SEMESTER COURSE	GR	HR	PT	YR	SECOND SEMESTER COURSE	GR	HR	PT	YR

Cook, Herman

Date Entered August 29, 1955
Date Born July 22, 1955
Graduated
Left Dec. 1956
Cause
Address 415 East Brainard St.
Phone

Washington Junior College partial transcript for Herman C. Cook, 1955. Courtesy of Pensacola State College.

Herman "Junior" Cook, third from right. Pictured with unidentified group, likely fellow students at Booker T. Washington Junior College, Pensacola, Florida. Undated photo, mid-1950s. Photo courtesy of Pensacola State College.

Horace Silver, Junior Cook, Gene Taylor, Blue Mitchell, Louis Hayes au Club Saint-Germain.

Birdland. J'étais très copain avec le patron : Oscar Goodstin. Je pouvais travailler mon piano tous les après-midi dans ce club. Chaque fois qu'il engageait un musicien qui n'avait pas sa propre formation, il lui recommandait de me prendre comme pianiste ou même de me charger de lui trouver des musiciens.

C'est ainsi que j'ai travaillé au Birdland avec Bill Harris, Chubby Jackson et Serge Chaloff. J'ai travaillé aussi avec Slim Gaillard, Kai Winding, et Terry Gibbs.

J'ai joué aussi au Birdland, avec mon idole Prez, pendant trois ou quatre mois : ce fut une expérience inoubliable. Non seulement Prez était un musicien fantastique, un innovateur, mais c'était aussi une personnalité unique. Il fallait connaître son langage, ses expressions, sa propre façon de s'exprimer... J'ai joué aussi avec ce géant qu'était Coleman Hawkins. J'ai travaillé, toujours au Birdland, avec Miles, avec lequel j'ai aussi enregistré. C'est un type extraordinaire à tous les points de vue, pas du tout ce que beaucoup de gens croient...

J'ai passé quelques mois avec Tony Scott et à peu près le même temps avec Eddie « Lockjaw » Davis. Puis, pour la première fois, j'ai présenté, toujours au Birdland, ma propre formation : Hank Mobley, Doug Watkins, Arthur Edgehill et moi-même. C'est durant cet engagement que je composai et enregistrai, pour la première fois, **Doodlin** et **The Preacher** (3).

C'est à ce moment précis qu'est né le groupe des Jazz Messengers (3) avec Mobley, Kenny Dorham, Doug, Blakey et moi-même. L'orchestre était organisé sur le modèle coopératif (comme le M.J.Q.). Nous nous partagions les responsabilités musicales et commerciales et cela a très bien marché pendant un an ! Ensuite nous nous sommes dispersés et Art Blakey a gardé le nom : « Jazz Messengers. »

J'ai formé mon groupe, celui qui a fait tant de disques pour Blue Note, immédiatement après avoir quitté les Jazz Messengers.

Un de nos succès les plus durables et les plus populaires fut **Señor Blues** que j'ai enregistré avec Donald Byrd, Mobley, Doug, Louis Hayes (4). Señor Blues eut un tel succès que je l'enregistrai aussi en 45 tours avec un vocal de Bill Henderson. J'avais, en effet, écrit des paroles sur ce thème (5). C'est une rareté discographique. Pour en revenir à ce qui se passait au Birdland, à cette époque, j'ai eu la chance de jouer et d'enregistrer avec Art Blakey et Clifford Brown. Nous avons travaillé deux ou trois semaines au Birdland. L'orchestre se composait de Clifford Brown, de Lou Donaldson, de moi-même, de Curley Russell et de Art Blakey. Nous avions tous entendu parler de Clifford Brown qui jusqu'alors n'était pas encore venu à New York. Il était originaire de Delaware.

Nous ne cessions de parler de ce fantastique trompettiste. Art Blakey lui a téléphoné et lui a demandé de venir faire ce gig. Pendant notre engagement au Birdland, Alfred Lyon et Francis Wolf, les deux fondateurs de Blue Note décidèrent de nous enregistrer en direct dans le club. Cela se passait en février 1954 (6). Henri Renaud, qui venait tous les soirs, a assisté à cette session. Un autre soir Miles est venu faire le « bœuf ». Nous essayâmes de rester ensemble et nous pûmes décrocher encore un gig d'une semaine à Philadelphie. Mais après, comme il n'y avait plus de travail, nous dûmes, la rage au cœur, nous séparer...

C'est à ce moment-là que Clifford Brown partit avec Max Roach en Californie où Max avait un engagement.

⁂

Mais revenons à l'époque où j'ai quitté l'orchestre que nous avions formé Art Blakey et moi, l'orchestre des Jazz Messengers. J'ai toujours recherché des musiciens qui aimaient ma musique, des musiciens qui se retrempent sans cesse dans le terreau de la musique négro-américaine, des musiciens pour lesquels la gospel music et les blues constituent l'idiome de base.

Prenons, par exemple, Silver Blue (7), c'est tout simplement le bon vieux blues traditionnel tout simple, joué, pour ainsi dire, en Jam Session, en si bémol. C'est le blues et non pas une certaine ligne mélodique construite sur les accords du blues traditionnel.

C'est tout simple... non ? C'est le genre de truc que j'adore. Mais, bien entendu, je ne me suis jamais limité à n'être qu'un pianiste-compositeur-arrangeur-chef d'orchestre étiqueté churchy, bluesy, funky ou soul. Cela ne constitue qu'une partie de la personnalité musicale d'Horace Silver. C'est bien sûr la partie qui est comme du grand public, qui m'a assuré un succès durable et certain. Mais il me semble qu'Horace Silver est, **en outre,** marqué par ce qui dans son œuvre est latin (8), folk, jazz, musique d'inspiration arabe, juive, orientale, africaine, extrême-orientale et jusqu'à la musique occidentale dite classique.

J'ai beaucoup aimé le Maroc où j'ai passé des vacances et où j'ai écouté beaucoup de musique. J'ai d'excellents rapports avec des musiciens d'Afrique du Sud, comme Myriam Makeba et Hugh Massakela.

De toute façon les musiciens que j'engage doivent être aptes à jouer toute ma musique, depuis les blues et les thèmes rappelant la gospel music... jusqu'à des compositions, en apparence au moins, assez éloignées de ces conceptions.

(Propos recueillis au magnétophone par Maurice Cullaz.)

(3) Horace Silver and the Jazz Messengers. Blue Note 1518.

(4) Horace Silver Quintet. Blue Note 1539.
(5) 45 tours Blue Note 45-1710.
(6) A night at Birdland. Blue Note BLP 1521 et 1522.

(7) The Horace Silver Quintet. EPIC-L.A. 16.005.
(8) Au sens américain du mot musique afro-cubaine, sud-américaine, antillaise.

24

Horace Silver Quintet, with Junior Cook on tenor saxophone, pictured in *Jazz Hot* magazine (Paris), no. 329, July–August 1976, p. 24.

jim harrison hilly saunders & jesse white
present

12 HOUR—12 TENOR

SAXOPHONE MARATHON

Saturday, October 25, 1969

6 P.M. TO 6 A.M.

FEATURING

TINA BROOKS	GEORGE COLEMAN
JUNIOR COOK	BOOKER ERVIN
FRANK FOSTER	BILLY HARPER
JIMMY HEATH	BILLY MITCHELL
SAM RIVERS	CHARLIE ROUSE
HAROLD VICK	FRANK WESS

PLUS 3 ALL STAR RHYTHM SECTIONS

MASTER OF CEREMONIES —
Ed Williams and Al Roberts WLIB—FM

CLUB AFRO-DISIAC

Tickets: $4.00 in advance —$5.00 at door

Advance Tickets at:

"A Jazz Spotlite Production"

JAZZ is ALIVE and WELL in NEW YORK

Advertisement for a "12 hour–12 tenor" Saxophone Marathon concert, Club Afro-Disiac, Jamaica, Queens, NYC, 25 October 1969. Courtesy of the Institute of Jazz Studies, John Cotton Dana Library, Rutgers University, Newark, New Jersey.

Junior Cook, circa 1976, probably in Italy. Photo by Luisa Cairati. Courtesy of the Institute of Jazz Studies photograph collection (IJS-0048), Rutgers.

Junior Cook, circa 1976. Probably Italy. Photo by Luisa Cairati. Courtesy of the Institute of Jazz Studies photograph collection (IJS-0048), Rutgers.

Louis Hayes–Junior Cook Quintet in Italy, circa 1976. *Left to right*: Stafford James, Woody Shaw, unidentified woman, Junior Cook, Ronnie Mathews, Maxine Gregg, unidentified woman, unidentified man. Photo by Luisa Cairati. Courtesy of the Institute of Jazz Studies photograph collection (IJS-0048), Rutgers.

Junior Cook and Bill Hardman, New York Jazz Museum, August 1977. Photo courtesy of Roseline Hardman.

Bill Hardman, Junior Cook, and Mickey Tucker at NY Jazz Museum, August 1977. Courtesy of Mickey and Sheila Tucker.

Hardman–Cook quintet rehearsal at the New Jersey home of Mickey Tucker. *Left to right*: Chin Suzuki, Junior Cook, Bill Hardman, Mickey Tucker, Eddie Gladden. Courtesy of Mickey and Sheila Tucker.

Junior Cook and Beatrice "Bea" Henellin, November 1977, at Mickey and Sheila Tucker's apartment on the Tuckers' wedding day. Courtesy of Mickey and Sheila Tucker.

Mickey and Sheila Tucker's wedding day, November 1977. *Left to right*: Grady Tate, Diane Goldsmith, Pete Brown, Sheila Tucker, Junior Cook. Courtesy of Mickey and Sheila Tucker.

Junior Cook with fans (unidentified) in the Netherlands, 1977.
Courtesy of Mickey and Sheila Tucker.

Junior Cook and Victor Jones (drums) on a gig in Sweden, 1977.
Courtesy of Mickey and Sheila Tucker.

Bill Hardman and Junior Cook, Muse Records publicity shot, 1978.
Photo by Josef Werkmeister. Courtesy of Roseline Hardman.

Bill Hardman (trumpet), Chin Suzuki (bass, obscured),
Junior Cook (saxophone), Hidelsheim, Germany, 1978.
Photo courtesy of Roseline Hardman.

Mickey Tucker (piano), Bill Hardman (trumpet), probably Chin Suzuki (bass), Junior Cook (tenor saxophone), drummer obscured. Hidelsheim, Germany, 1978. Photo courtesy of Roseline Hardman.

Junior Cook and Bill Hardman, New York City, 1978. Photo courtesy of Roseline Hardman.

Herman "Junior" Cook, C. I. Recording Studio, NYC, after recording Mickey Tucker's *The Crawl*, 1979. Courtesy of Mickey and Sheila Tucker.

Left to right: Junior Cook, Mickey Tucker, Dexter Gordon. Photo by Mitchell Seidel. Courtesy of Mickey and Sheila Tucker.

Left to right: Junior Cook, Mickey Tucker, Roseline Hardman, unidentified woman, unidentified woman, Sheila Tucker. Courtesy of Mickey and Sheila Tucker.

Left to right: Junior Cook, Bill Hardman, and Slide Hampton, probably at the New York Jazz Museum. Courtesy of Mickey and Sheila Tucker.

Bill Hardman and Junior Cook (*foreground*) performing in Hartford, Connecticut, June 1980. Courtesy of Roseline Hardman.

Junior Cook, performing aboard the Jazzmobile (New York City), circa 1986. Photo by David Spitzer.

Junior Cook, performing aboard the Jazzmobile (New York City), circa 1986. Photo by David Spitzer.

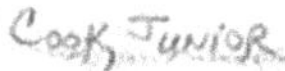

—-for Valentines Day

" BACK BY POPULAR DEMAND "

Junior Cook

AND

Bill Hardman

Quintet

EXTRA ADDED ATTRACTION

SPECIAL GUEST vocalists

SUZANNE KLEWAN
&TIMMY SHEPHERD

FRIDAY, SATURDAY, February 14th 15th 1986

Three Shows Nightly
10pm 11:30pm 1am

ADMISSION $6.00 ADV. / $8.00 DOOR

Senior citizens and students with Identification $5.00

RESERVATIONS REQUIRED
FOR ADVANCE PRICE

Food and non-alcoholic beverages served

GROUP DISCOUNTS AVAILABLE

Flyer for Bill Hardman–Junior Cook Quintet gig at Jazz Cultural Theatre, NYC, 1986. Courtesy of the Institute of Jazz Studies, Rutgers.

Flyer for Junior Cook and other performances at Condon's jazz club, NYC, date unspecified. Courtesy of the Institute of Jazz Studies, Rutgers.

Star Café, New York City. Photo courtesy of Michael Wiess.

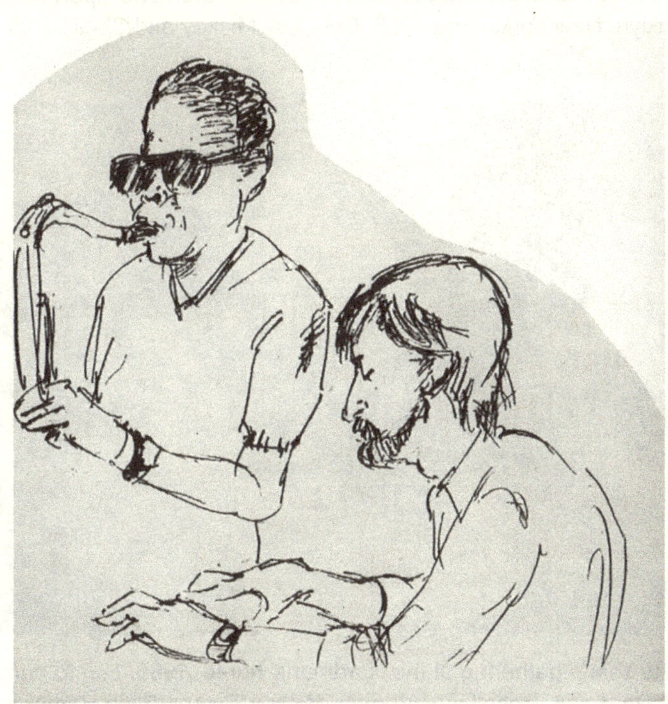

Drawing of Junior Cook (saxophone) and Michael Weiss (piano), depiction from the Star Café, dated 1984. Artist unknown. Photo courtesy of Michael Weiss.

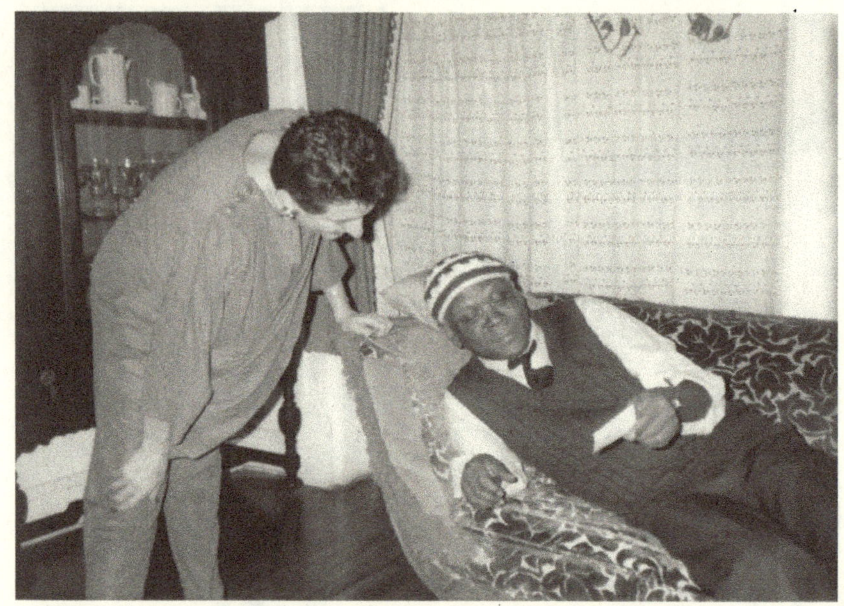

Roseline Hardman and Junior Cook at the Hardmans' apartment, Brooklyn, New York, circa 1986. Courtesy Mickey and Sheila Tucker.

New Year's gathering at the Hardmans' home, 1986. *Left to right*: Bill Hardman, Roseline Hardman, Mickey Tucker, Slide Hampton, unidentified woman, Beatrice Henellin, Junior Cook. Photo courtesy of Roseline Hardman.

Beatrice Henellin and Junior Cook, January 1986.
Photo courtesy of Roseline Hardman.

Left to right: Michael Weiss, Junior Cook, (bassist obscured), Bill Hardman, unidentified drummer. Performing at New Morning, Paris, France, 1986.
Photo courtesy of Roseline Hardman.

Sheila Tucker, Junior Cook, Bill Hardman, May 1986.
Courtesy of Mickey and Sheila Tucker.

Michael Weiss (piano), and Peter Washington (bass), Flamingo Lounge, NYC, 1987. Junior Cook is on the gig but not pictured. Courtesy of Michael Weiss.

Left to right: Bassist obscured, Clifford Barbaro (drums), Michael Weiss (piano), Junior Cook (saxophone), Timmy Shepherd (vocals), and Bill Hardman (trumpet), Village Gate jazz club, 1987. Photo courtesy of Michael Weiss.

Vocalist Timmy Shepherd and the author, September 2024.

Junior Cook at the Tuckers' Apartment in New Jersey.
Courtesy of Mickey and Sheila Tucker.

Left to right: Junior Cook (saxophone), Michael Weiss (piano), Peter Washington (bass), drummer unidentified, Bradley's piano bar, NYC, 25 June 1989. Picture courtesy of Michael Weiss.

Left to right: Junior Cook, Mickey Tucker, and Irene Reid, Melbourne, Australia, October 1991. Courtesy of Mickey and Sheila Tucker.

Junior Cook (*second from left*) and Mickey Tucker (*right*) with friends, Melbourne, Australia, October 1991. Courtesy of Mickey and Sheila Tucker.

Undated photo of Junior Cook, probably mid- to late 1980s publicity shot. Photographer unknown. Courtesy of Mickey and Sheila Tucker.

- INTERMENT -
Restland Memorial Park
East Hanover, New Jersey

ACKNOWLEDGEMENT
The Family wishes to express their deep gratitude for the comforting words, prayers and other acts of kindness.

Funeral Arrangements entrusted to:

JOHN H. JOYCE, INC.
Funeral Directors
2332 Adam Clayton Powell Jr., Blvd.
New York, N.Y. 10030
212-690-3500

In Loving Memory of

HERMAN "JR" COOK

1934 - 1992

Monday, February 10, 1992

11:00 A.M.

Order of Service

Organ Prelude

Processional

Prayer of Comfort

Selection

Eulogy — Reverend Gensel

Benediction

Recessional

Organ Postlude

Obituary

Jr Cook was a man of few words who dedicated his life to music. The saxophone was not only a musical instrument, but his means of communicating with the world. The magic of his music conveyed the love and joy he had in his heart.

Jr Cook's style lifted him into a class by himself. The vastness and originality of his contribution to our lives and to the world of jazz is eternal.

Jr Cook was not only a musician, he was a humanitarian and a teacher. He has and will continue to inspire musicians for generations to come.

Jr Cook is survived by Mr. and Mrs. Robert Cook and Mr. and Mrs. John Cook, as well as a large family, lots of loving friends and all those who have been lucky enough to enjoy his music over the years.

Those of us who know Jr Cook know that he lives through the legacy of the music he created.

Copy of funeral program for Herman "Junior" Cook, 10 February 1992. Courtesy of Patricia Landry.

Grave site marker, Restland Memorial Park, East Hanover, New Jersey.
Photo by the author.

Chapter 5

Shout Chorus

All I can do is have my music together when I get out there. I never expected to be rich or famous, but I have the respect of my peers. That's enough. I'm still doing what I set out to do, playing this music.
—Herman "Junior" Cook, October 1991[1]

Shout Chorus

Musicians, producers, and friends in over a dozen interviews summarized Cook's music and contribution, his sound, and his personality with vivid descriptors and phrases. These tell the story of Herman "Junior" Cook.

Golden sound
Laid-back
Big, fat, long tones
Intensity
Deep rooted bebop but stuff never heard before
He just played his fucking ass off
Man of few words
Swinging

Robust
Strident
Honest musician
The Majors
Expressive
Lyricism
Relaxed
Fire
Beautiful melody
Kicking ass
'Trane changes but his own shit
Very much kept to himself
Fluid
In the trenches
Brawny
Economical
True improviser
Gut level
Warmth
Precision

What *was* Junior Cook's sound? Ratliff defined a musician's sound as "a full and sensible embodiment of [the musician's] musical personality, such that it can be heard, at best, in a single note."[2] Knowing the voices of one's family members is an apt analogy: When my close relatives call on the phone, they don't have to identify themselves. I know from the first words, mentally identify the caller—my mom, or my aunt, or one of my siblings, or close friends—and jump right into conversation. What is it about those callers, and everything that makes up their sound, that allows me to identify them? The timbre and pitch of their voice, their word choices (my mom answers my "Hello" on the phone sometimes by singing a piece of an old jingle), or the inflection and length of their words and phrases (my cousin's "Hi" is a middle-C, staccato greeting, whereas my dad's "HELL-oh," leaned in and drawled out, demonstrated his eagerness for dialogue).

What were the characteristics that allow us to recognize Junior Cook's sound? What made his saxophone voice unique? His was always a round sound, of the Mobley mold. His tone was very direct and present, almost to the point of breaking, like the ring of a strummed guitar string just on the clean side of distortion. Saxophonist Lalama also pegged Mobley as a reference point for Cook's improvisations; like Mobley, Cook's solos had "everything in its right place." Lalama also asserted that Cook's playing was characterized by "never a wrong or stupid note"; that is, they carried weight and were not extraneous.[3] Trumpeter Ponomarev underscored Cook's precision, which is quite a feat for a jazz musician reportedly not content to play musical cliches and stock phrases and is a nod to Cook's technical proficiency.[4] Mickey Tucker, known for his own technical virtuosity in playing and in composition, affirmed that Cook was his favorite saxophonist and that Cook could handle every piece of music that Tucker put in front of him.[5] Though Cook's playing seemed slightly biased for the middle and upper range of the saxophone, he had full command of the horn, accessing both altissimo and the lower register in his solos. It was very rare that his solos would feature trills, false fingerings, or less structured sound, though there are a few examples, such as the third chorus of his solo on Blue Mitchell's "Fungi Mama," where his trilly shakes do conjure Joe Henderson.

Many accounts peg Junior Cook simplistically as hard bop, and leave him there. For example, Herb Wong's liner notes for *Two Tenor Winner* (Cook and Clifford Jordan; Criss Cross, 1984) asserted that Cook, a "consistent performer," had "never really departed from the intelligent post-bop style that launched him as a respected professional" in the late 1950s. An October 1991 press review of Cook's visit to Australia teed up the topic by saying that he "has played in essentially the same hard bop style for the past 30 years or so."[6]

Cook was deep in the hard bop style, but the generalizations also understate the arc of his approach across a spectrum that started with his R&B beginnings, rose to notoriety with the bluesy discipline of Silver's hard bop approach, and proceeded to explore a looser Trane-chasing fluidity with Hubbard and Hayes before mashing the Trane fluidity and 1960's discipline without fully returning to the Silver-era variant. For example, Cook's treatment of the jazz standard "All the Things You Are" over a decade or so provides a lens for comparison.

Three recordings of Cook playing "All the Things You Are"—with the Hayes–Cook quintet in Hamburg, Germany (1976),[7] with the Kenny Drew quartet in Tokyo, Japan (1981),[8] and with the Hardman–Cook quintet in Paris, France (1986)[9]—demonstrate Cook's evolution over that period. The 1981 and 1986 recordings appear similar in approach, whereas the 1976 recording highlights Cook under the sway of Coltrane, reaching more urgently for more musical statements, seemingly at once.

Pianist David Hazeltine pointed to Horace Silver, and his specific vision for his band's sound, as a significant influence on Cook's playing: "At the time Junior played with Horace Silver, that was a very specific band and it was continuing in the tradition of the Horace Silver quintet and Junior played conservatively in that [band], whereas when he played with Freddie and later years, he . . . I think he was more . . . you could say 'experimental' in what he wanted to play."[10] *DownBeat*'s Barbara Gardner, in the magazine's feature of Horace Silver in 1963, said that "in performance, the group is a supreme example of disciplined abandonment in music." She wrote that each musician in the group is "considered an excellent technician and a driving expressionist in his own right" and that they consciously craft their music in deference to Silver's vision: "There is no mistaking the ownership of the group. It is a Horace Silver unit from first to last note. It reflects the leader's driving, smoking intensity, but each member contributes to that unit-feel."[11] Thus, Silver likely influenced Junior Cook's improvisational approach in a similar way that Richard Cook in his Blue Note biography noted that Silver's band compelled Joe Henderson to play a more conservative, more tame, version of his "natural," organic musical inclinations.[12]

****

All in all, Cook could play. He played well, in bands that garnered the attention of jazz audiences through the years. So, then, why isn't Cook better known in jazz history?

Jazz audiences and musicians may be prone to overlook Cook's contribution to the music because his improvisational acumen was not coupled with a repertoire of original music. Here we can return to Joe Henderson for comparison. Henderson's jazz career highlighted both his playing and his pen—"Recordame," "Punjab," "Isotope," "Inner Urge," and several of his other compositions are mainstays in the jazz canon. Mobley, slightly Cook's senior, also contributed several tunes that are now standards in the jazz repertoire—"No Room for Squares," "A Caddy for Daddy," "Soul Station," "My Groove, Your Move," and the stalwart "This I Dig of You." Cook made no such compositional contributions to the repertoire of jazz standards. Recall jazz producer Cuscuna's explanation of the importance of compositions to the popularity of Silver's quintet and of other groups: "In those days, it was all about the tunes."[13]

Cook's career also likely generated less notoriety relative to others in part because he did not skate the jazz rink as a leader but, rather, as a sideman in other musicians' bands. Cook predominantly led a sideman's life; he was on the stage, to be sure, but not necessarily in the spotlight. Society, though, especially American society, in many cases favors the spotlight, favors the leaders. Most other Silver tenorists, for example—Mobley, Henderson, Brecker, Berg—went on to build careers as solo artists, bandleaders in their own right.

Journalist and jazz critic Ratliff noted in this way that playing your axe and arranging tunes is not the end but just the beginning of many of the most successful careers in jazz. Beyond the music, many successful leaders must marshal organizational skills to put a band together; emotional skills to keep a band together; interpersonal skills to choose the right talent and personalities to share a stage, to network, and to impress club owners and record label executives with their potential; administrative skills to book the gigs out there; and even the entrepreneurial skills to establish gigs where none previously existed. The skills mix, said Ratliff, is "like going through the eyes of multiple needles."[14] Saxophonist Lakecia Benjamin in a July 2024 interview spoke of these various skills when remarking on her observations while on tour with jazz trumpet legend Clark Terry: "Watching him [Terry] as a bandleader . . . how amazing he was at the trumpet and his chops, but how good he was at dealing with the audience, how good he was at . . . dressed to the nines. You know, I really saw from him just a lot of what it was going to take to . . . you know, besides the music, to be amazing."[15] To acknowledge Cook's seeming lack of broad business acumen does not take away from him as a musician but provides a view of the multiple layers of a so-called successful jazz career and of an industry and audience that managed to miss him, or at least not focus its attention on him, even as Cook made the roster for some of the idiom's best bands over decades.

It's also possible that the "hard bop" moniker cast a bit of a shadow on his career. David Rosenthal, in his essay "Hard Bop and Its Critics," notes that hard bop as a category received more than its share of disdain among critics, highlighting that *DownBeat* magazine's critics from 1955 to 1965 held views on hard bop that "verged on the hysterical."[16] Critics' general diminution of the hard bop contribution seemed in some cases to have extended to its most ardent practitioners. For example, John S. Wilson, writing for the *New York Times* (4 April 1970), described the Freddie Hubbard Sextet (including Cook on tenor and Cedar Walton on piano) as "one of the most polished exemplars of a style that is a heritage of the be-bop era of 25 years ago." Following that intro, however, he caustically summarized the style as "[involving] highly competent musicians playing an emotionally static music in which one note coldly follows another with scarcely any sense of dynamics or emotional involvement."[17]

Of course, Wilson's critique also highlights the futility of attempts to categorize the genre and the inherent difficulty in establishing the parameters of one genre in the jazz idiom. Wilson did not explicitly identify the style that he described. Is he describing hard bop, the genre-style of "Moanin'" (Bobby Timmons, 1958), "Cool Eyes" (Horace Silver, 1956), "One for Daddy-O" (Cannonball Adderly, 1958), "Christo Redentor" (Duke Pearson, 1964), and "Tanya" (Donald Byrd, 1964)? Surely, those tunes are neither "emotionally static" nor lacking "any sense of dynamics or emotional involvement." Bill Pierce expressed his personal disdain for the "hard bop" descriptor during an interview for this work; jazz writer Doug Ramsey similarly lamented the "hard bop" descriptor as an example of "box theory" in music, humans' urge to put ideas in a box.[18]

Rosenthal writes, "unfortunately, hard bop has had many detractors and few articulate defenders; and perhaps, for this reason, many critical opinions have come to be accepted as received wisdom."[19] Countering those "critical opinions," Rosenthal affirmed hard bop's staying power by highlighting that many "new releases" of the time period in which he wrote (the 1980s) were actually "reissues of sides cut during the 1955–1965 years, and most of these are hard bop dates."[20]

Even now many present-day jazz titans (saxophonists Ralph Moore, Vincent Herring, Eric Alexander, Javon Jackson; pianist Benny Green) arguably exhibit a clear hard bop sensibility. The late Roy Hargrove's peppy compositions "Strasbourg St. Denis" and "Crazy Race," Jon Baptiste's "BLACCK," Maurice Brown's "Time Tick Tock," Joshua Redman's "Freedom in the Groove"—all carry that inviting, bluesy, don't-just-listen-to-us, come-on-in-and-groove-with-us character. My own introduction to Junior Cook came from seeking out Horace Silver's original *Live at the Village Gate* release after hearing a cover of Silver's "Kiss Me Right" on the Harper Brothers' disc *Remembrance: Live at the Village Vanguard* (Verve Records), which was released in 1990.

Cook ably played the game, but he admittedly did not change the game—another possible demerit in the industry and public eye and attention span. He was not a pioneer, as were the vanguard musicians like Bird and Dizzy and Monk, who led jazz out of big-band-swing and into the bebop thing. He did not, like Coltrane, introduce new, complex chord progressions ("Trane changes"), popularize the torrential so-called sheets of sound, or resurrect the soprano saxophone. Cook was not the first to stretch the range of the saxophone with altissimo alternate fingerings to reach higher pitches on the horn. As noted previously, he did not write new tunes or song forms into the jazz canon. He did not introduce new or lesser-used instruments into the music or play multiple instruments at once, a la Rahsaan Roland Kirk. From Ratliff again, "structural newness" and "genre newness" may not have been Cook's claims to fame, but rather his "genuinely individual expression"—valuable in itself—both acknowledged the past and built on that past in the present.[21] Cook's authentic, individual musical expressions were the bricks that helped build a jazz genre. After all, cornerstones are necessary to build a structure, but an edifice with only cornerstones is no edifice.

Cook, to be sure, also lived and performed among a crowded field of virtuoso practitioners of the jazz tenor. In an interview for this work, producer Michael Cuscuna named John Coltrane, Sonny Rollins, Junior Cook, Clifford Jordan, Tina Brooks, Roland Alexander, Stanley Turrentine, and Jimmy

Heath, just hitting the tip of the iceberg with respect to what he described as the "wealth of talent in the 1960s" on saxophone.[22] To consider those who would have been numbered among Cook's peers in the music is to begin to appreciate the boundless creativity on the scene; many of them, including Cook, were of course centered in New York City. Dexter Gordon, the elder statesman of the time, was born in 1923. Sonny Stitt was born a year later, 1924. Gene Ammons was born in 1925. John Coltrane and Jimmy Heath both were born in 1926. Stan Getz was born in 1927. Johnny Griffin and Harold Land both were born in 1928. Stanley Turrentine, King Curtis, Eddie Harris, and Houston Person all were born in 1934, the same year as Cook. The roster of Cook's age-peer contemporaries on tenor saxophone, born within plus or minus five years of his birth, is staggering:

Birth Year	Name
1929	Benny Golson
1930	Hank Mobley, Sonny Rollins, Ornette Coleman
1931	Clifford Jordan, Dewey Redman
1932	Gato Barbieri, Tina Brooks
1933	Wayne Shorter
1934	Stanley Turrentine, **Junior Cook**, Curtis "King Curtis" Osley, Eddie Harris, Houston Person
1935	George Coleman, Tubby Hayes, Rahsaan Roland Kirk
1936	Albert Ayler, Nick Brignola, Harold Vick
1937	Bootsie Barnes, Gordon Brisker, Joe Henderson, Archie Shepp
1938	Charles Lloyd, Sal Nistico, Odean Pope
1939	Sonny Fortune

Cook spent the last ten or so years of his life centered in New York City, never without his horn, leading jam sessions and as featured guest on gigs at a bevy of clubs and rooms, many of which have long since faded away: the Star Café (Twenty-Third Street), Augie's, Flamingo Lounge, Paris (Washington Heights), Boomer's, Condon's, Fat Tuesdays, Sweet Basil's, Joyce's, the Village Vanguard (still around), the Village Gate, the Angry Squire, Fez (East Village), the Blue Note (still around), the Baby Grand (uptown, 319 West 125th Street), the Jazz Forum (50 Cooper Square), Dude's Lounge (uptown),

Visiones, Cooper Union's Great Hall (Seventh Street and Third Avenue), Bradley's (70 University Place), Salt Peanuts (399 Greenwich Street, with the tag line in magazine ads, "Be Bop Preserved Here"), Sue's Place (Brooklyn), the West End Café, the Red Rooster, the Lickety Split, the Blue Cornet (Brooklyn), Jazz Cultural Theatre (Eighth Avenue between Twenty-Eighth and Twenty-Ninth Streets), the Jazzmania Society (14 East Twenty-Third Street), the Tin Palace, Zanzibar (Second Avenue), the Blue Book (145th), the Knickerbocker, Surf Maid (151 Bleecker Street, now the Red Lion), Olympic Towers Atrium, Prospect Park Bandshell (Brooklyn), Billy's.

Cook's contribution to the idiom, according to Moore, was in part his dedication to community and to building a community of jazz practitioners the "old fashioned way" through apprenticeship–"osmosis," as Tardo Hammer recalled. "The greats came up in community," Moore summarized, "and worked out what they could from records and from listening to each other at gigs."[23] That community was live and in person. Cook sought relationship among musicians and relationship within the music, which, in that time period, was all that was available: there was no YouTube, with its international repository of concerts and masterclasses, no play-along series to practice one's craft at home like those made famous by saxophonist and educator Jamey Aebersold, no books of patterns and enclosures written in twelve keys. One wonders how YouTube and play-alongs and pattern books in the present era—spreading the music and jazz education in isolation—may be degrading the sense of community, of mentor-protégé, and of relationship that Cook championed and that advanced the idiom for most of the first century of jazz's existence. Moore exhaled in passing, "Jazz has gone to school now," and in so doing, the face, heart, and soul of the music has changed.[24]

To ask why Junior Cook was not better known and regarded in the jazz industry and jazz history leads toward a discussion of what constitutes a successful jazz career—a question with as many answers as interrogators and practitioners. From accounts and anecdotes, it is clear that Cook's life was not without disappointment. He was not without some hard times, personal and professional. Nevertheless, he persisted. A jazz Jeremiah, he had the "respect of his peers" and did what he "set out to do, playing this music," according to his own remarks in a 1991 interview.[25] He succeeded. Now, this interpretation is not intended to lower the bar for what constitutes a "successful" jazz career; it is not intended to bestow upon Cook an effort grade and raise his hand in the air in victory. It recognizes a life devoted to music, devoted to practice, devoted to showing up. As the old saying goes, when you run a marathon, people don't often ask your finishing time; more often they ask, "Did you finish?" recognizing that steadfast perseverance is itself an accomplishment and appreciating that, ultimately, the race is against oneself. The twentieth-century birth and growth of the jazz idiom taught us that the practice of jazz is built on continuity. The success of Cook's career and life was built on the same continuity, from the family musical influences of his childhood, weaving through Ray Shep and the Pensacola music scene, Gigi Gryce, intertwining in R&B, immersed in Horace Silver and New York City, hard bop, fusion, quintets, large gigs, small gigs, big bands, ovations and encores, gigs cut short because there were no patrons, the '80s doldrums, the '90s revivals, jam sessions, and after-hours sessions, all the way to the last bars of his life.

What does a sideman's life reveal about leadership? Is a sideman's life representative of leadership if the sideman is not in the spotlight? Can a sideman's life be regarded as leadership? Of course it can. We live our lives in multiple spheres simultaneously. Cook's comparative lack of marquee billing (i.e., "leader dates," gigs as leader of an ensemble) does not detract from his leadership on the jam session bandstand at the Star Café and Augie's, nor does it detract from his leadership as a sideman. Were Justin Robinson (alto saxophone) and Gerald Clayton (piano) not leaders when they supported Roy Hargrove's unstoppable groove in Hargrove's own band? (Who is leading Roy Hargrove's band when Gerald Clayton is soloing? Gerald Clayton is.) Sure, there is still Roy Hargrove without Robinson and Clayton, but there is no Roy Hargrove group, no Roy Hargrove band, without Robinson or Clayton or Bruce Williams (alto saxophone) or Jason Marshall (baritone saxophone) or Reggie Washington or Lenny Stallworth (both bass) or Renee Neufville (vocals) or a young Jon Batiste (piano) or some assemblage of sidemen and sidewomen.

Society (especially American society) and jazz history nonetheless will see what it wants to see—the leaders on the date, the marquee billing, the entrepreneurs, the innovators, those in the spotlight and on society's Olympic trilevel podiums for every category of everything. The *New York Times'* Roxane Orgill declared in a 1996 article about saxophonist Steve Wilson that "anonymity is a fact of life for a jazz sideman."[26]

Some of Cook's friends and fellow musicians cast him as a tragic figure, incredulous at how he made it in the meat grinder environment of New York City. Tenor saxophonist Ralph Moore lamented "how New York would treat" Cook and many other players, especially during the 1970s and early 1980s, some of New York City's darkest days.[27] Yet Cook lived, and he played.

Who was Herman "Junior" Cook? Cook was among the best-known tenorists that jazzers don't really know. Born and raised in Pensacola, formed on the road, and molded in New York, Cook was the woodwind in the sails of many of jazz history's great bands. Gone, but not forgotten.

Outro

I Lyfted with anticipation from Rutgers University's Newark campus to Restland Memorial Park in East Hanover, New Jersey. The Lyft pulled in to the entrance. "RESTLAND" in white background with cutout lettering, stencil-like, reminded me of an old Howard County, Maryland, amusement park of the 1970s. No pomp, no flash, just a clear, quiet confirmation that you have reached your destination.

A pleasant young lady, Marlene, met me outside and brought me in the office to bestow upon me the tools to find Junior Cook's gravesite. "Come right in and we will help you find your loved one," she offered, and disappeared around a corner and into an inner room.

"Loved one." She'd said that the day before on the phone. Did I need to correct her? Did she presume me to be a blood relative? I love Junior Cook's playing, but we are not related. He never knew me from a can of paint. Yet here I was, a train ride from my beloved Washington, DC, and a Lyft from Newark to find the final resting place of a man I've known only through audio recordings. An odyssey for information. A quest for closure.

The lobby just inside the office door was neat and unoffending. White walls, a picture of the park chapel. Autumnal hued flowers were in a vase in one corner and, opposite, American flags leaning at parade rest in a cannister awaiting the next remembrance. Two armchairs complemented the flowers. The lobby had three entranceways, one each on the three walls opposite the entry door, allowing the staff choices in how to best proceed to meet their clients' needs.

"Marvin?" she inquired from maybe one and a half rooms over as I waited in the lobby.

"Herman," I answered.

"Oh, I'm sorry," she said. I quietly appreciated her gesture at making such an honest mistake.

"And he passed in 1992?"

"Yes, ma'am."

Marlene appeared again through an entranceway other than the one she had disappeared into just ninety-two seconds before. With a paper featuring a grid in one hand, she rummaged through a credenza file drawer for a map with the grace of knowing everything was right where she expected it to be. She reached for a magnifying glass and inspected the grid for the right location. She then outlined in yellow highlighter my next half hour and change.

"Here. F-190. Here is a map. You are here. You will walk this way, past the chapel, and off to the right to 'Woodside.' The grave site is here," pointing to the grid, "so you can see it's not very far in."

"Yes ma'am. Thank you very much for your help."

Back out in the dry, eighty-degree early fall day, I started down the road toward the site. The road to the chapel was a tree-lined, dual one-way road, the chapel itself a gray stone building with triangled roofs and stained-glass windows that denied their beauty to those outside, on the sun side. Crumbling aged mortar on the stones had been shored up and replaced as needed, showing like an Etch-a-Sketch on the building's walls. Around the chapel and down the way. The sections of the cemetery were delineated by tree names: Elm, Spruce, Birch. Eventually, "Woodside," the section I sought. Cook's section.

Treasure hunt, indeed. "F-190." I studied the grid. "F" would be the sixth row and on the far third of the row of grave sites. Rather than take the whole affair methodically, I dove in eagerly, bending down to clear semidamp, hay-colored grass from a marker. Inefficient, to say the least. I ventured to what appeared to be the corner of the grid and walked six rows as mosquitoes made appetizers of my arms. Then . . . down fourteen to F-190. But it wasn't Cook. In fact, after counting twelve, it almost seemed as if lots 13 and 14 were vacant. Was I in the wrong place? Or was the marker so overgrown with thirty years of sod? I looked, counted, recounted, and put my backpack down in the grass to offload the added weight. I inspected a few spots using my fingers to brush away damp grass only to find a name that wasn't Cook. I pressed my fingers into the ground to see if they would find a metal marker beneath moist dirt. It was 2:40 pm and the groundspeople were due to leave at 3:00, so I called the lifeline. Marlene answered, helpful as ever, and offered to dispatch someone to my location.

A few minutes later a white pickup arrived. A burly, Hagrid-looking fellow reviewed his notebook with laminated pages to zero in on the spot. "What's the location?"

"190."

"Row?"

"F."

He stepped out of the truck and walked assuredly into the section, to and through the spot that I had measured, one row over and two to four lots further in.

"Did he have a marker?"

"Um . . . I don't know."

"Well, we can keep looking unless this is it." With that he took the heel of his boot and with one backward swipe he uncovered enough sod to mark the search over. Peeking out beneath thick clover-dotted grass and brown earth was the gold outline, "COOK," against a black background.

"Next time, call ahead. We can have it all ready for you," the man offered and he returned to his truck and the remnant of his workday.

The comparisons were too easy. Cook's grave site was like much of his career in the jazz industry—overlooked, lost in the shuffle, crowded over, starving for more attention.

I was elated but still dispassionate in the find. Much like the biography project that set me on this journey, I put some elbow grease on his marker to make Cook's name and representation more visible. I dug my fingers into the semidamp sod, and it came apart with barely moderate effort. I ripped small clumps at a time around the edges; earthworms and a snail slithered out of the work zone. Clearing progressively around the edges, I found Cook's full name—Herman C. "Junior" Cook—birth and death dates, a gold tenor saxophone in the upper right corner, and a treble clef with two eighth notes, on B and C, in the lower left corner. A few spare napkins from breakfast at PJ's Coffee and water from my bottle helped clear away some of the grime of time. The marker's edge was beveled with a hammered finish, gold pitted with the marker's espresso background.

Here lies Herman "Junior" Cook. Pensacola-born. "Juicy Lucy's" Cook. "Sister Sadie's" Cook. Cook, who blew the blues away. "Señor Blues'" Cook. Herman C. Cook. "June Bug." Star Café stalwart.

Tenorist Javon Jackson said during an interview, "All we have now are the recordings."[1] Recordings and memories.

We live after we live. When our time on earth is done, we live in what we left: legacy, music, feelings, memories, or absence of memories, which sometimes can occupy even more space. We live in lore: Some remember only the good things and tend to exaggerate their importance. Others remember the bad things, the missteps, the faults and hold the person's memory at the same distance they held them in life.

Life is for living. And living makes a life. Thank God for the life of Herman "Junior" Cook. Rest in peace, "loved one."

Acknowledgments

Through social media sleuthing and networking, I connected with musicians and others who interacted with Cook on the stage, in the recording studio, in the classroom, or in life. I engaged in several cold calls, holding out faith that the individual's appreciation for Cook and their curiosity about this project might overcome the natural skepticism and dismissiveness toward a complete stranger calling them on the phone and requesting information. Most of the contacts returned my calls, were willing to share their memories, and were very generous with their time via phone, Zoom, FaceTime, or email interviews:

- Saxophonist Bill Pierce (Art Blakey and the Jazz Messengers alumnus) attended Berklee during Cook's teaching stint there.
- Pianist Mickey Tucker recorded with Cook and was part of the Bill Hardman–Junior Cook Quintet of the 1980s.
- Drummer Leroy Williams recorded with Cook and was part of the Hardman–Cook quintet (my phone interview with Williams took place about a month before he passed in June 2022).
- Nils Winther, founder of SteepleChase Records.
- Roseline Hardman, widow of trumpeter Bill Hardman.
- Vocalist Timmy Shepherd roomed with Cook for a few years in the 1980s. Conversations with the elder Shepherd, and his son, saxophonist Kelly Shepherd, especially expanded the palette available to me to paint this written portrait of Cook's life.
- Tenor saxophonist Javon Jackson, another Jazz Messengers alumnus, provided great context on his interactions with Cook in the last years of Cook's life.
- Roberto Romeo, instrument repair technician, apprentice to Saul Fromkin, and owner of Roberto's Winds in NYC.
- Tenor saxophonist Fred Daniels.
- Jazz drum legend Louis Hayes.

- Jazz pianist Michael Weiss, who played with Cook at the Star Café in New York City and was a member of the Bill Hardman–Junior Cook Quintet.
- Jazz trumpeter Valery Ponomarev, who played on Cook's last release, *You Leave Me Breathless*.
- Jazz producer and cofounder of Mosaic Records, Michael Cuscuna (passed in April 2024).
- Jazz drummer Joe Farnsworth, who led the jam session at Augie's jazz club in the last years of Cook's life.
- Jazz pianist David Hazeltine, who played at the Star Café jam session.
- Trumpeter Klaus-Werner Pusch, student of Bill Hardman.
- Trumpeter Mra Oma.
- Saxophonist and writer Su Terry.
- Pianist Tardo Hammer.
- Trumpeter Richie Vitale.
- Drummer Andre White, on the faculty at McGill University.
- Saxophonist Ralph Lalama, on the faculty at State University of New York (SUNY), Purchase.
- Tenor saxophonist and Horace Silver quintet alum Ralph Moore (Moore, much like Cook, played in groups with Silver and Freddie Hubbard, and subbed for Cook in the Hardman–Cook quintet).
- Augusta Quirk, friend of Junior Cook and frequent patron of the Augie's jam scene.
- Ben Ratliff, journalist, music critic, and author of *Coltrane: The Story of a Sound*, among other works.
- Maxine Gordon, widow of tenor saxophone legend Dexter Gordon, archivist, and jazz historian. Gordon (née Gregg) was road manager for the Louis Hayes–Junior Cook Quintet of the mid-1970s.
- Saxophonist and educator Tim Warfield, one of the "tough young tenors" to emerge in the industry in the 1990s.
- Trumpeter and jazz historian Muneer Nasser.
- Muhammed Bilal Abdullah, formerly known as Tyrone Washington, saxophonist who succeeded Joe Henderson in Horace Silver's mighty quintet.

- Newcastle, Australia–born drummer Andrew Dickeson.
- Jean Jones, resident of Pensacola, Florida, and classmate of Cook's older brother John.
- Pensacola-born multi-instrumentalist and music producer Joseph Herring.
- Patricia Landry, Boston resident and Cook companion.

I am indebted to these musicians and individuals for sharing their memories, their perspective, and, in some cases, their private collection of photos for this work. I also appreciate the assistance of Leann Purdy, records support specialist at Pensacola State College, who unearthed Cook's college enrollment records, adding a layer of detail to his Pensacola years. Jessie Cragg, curator of exhibits at the University of West Florida (UWF) Historic Trust, aided with a search of UWF holdings. The late F. Norman Vickers of the Jazz Society of Pensacola, saxophonist Joe Occhipinti, and the Jazz Room at West Florida Public Library (Pensacola, Florida) also provided early encouragement for this work. Thanks also to Mark Gilbert and *Jazz Journal* (UK) for the publication of an early appreciation of Cook based on research from this work ("Junior Cook: Quintessential NYC Hard-Bop Tenor"). Pianist Manuel Schmiedel helped me immensely by transcribing some Cook solos.

Primary sources unfortunately were not in plentiful supply. In some cases liner notes (a bit of a lost art) filled the gap. Liner notes were a staple of albums released in the twentieth century and seemingly all but forgotten in this current age where one purchases an album with the click of a button for digital download or streaming access. The album liner notes of the last century usually featured a writer, jazz critic, or producer—Ira Gitler, Leonard Feather, Ben Case, Delfeayo Marsalis—and sometimes the artist himself or herself, who set the context for the music. Liner notes often acknowledged the album's personnel while weaving in, interview-style, lesser-known highlights of the headliner's life and career. I discovered aspects of Cook's life and career that I hadn't read in any other references. Quotes from Cook himself presented the saxophonist's career and musical perspective in his own words.

Robin Reshard ("Her Highness") jumpstarted my research on Junior Cook's early years in Pensacola with a phenomenal research effort based on census data, city directories, and other sources. I am indebted to her selfless investment in this project. I also thank former UWF graduate students Sarah Fugarino and Mariah Hills, who responded to my cold call and helped me access the UWF-Jazz Society of Pensacola public history project on Pensacola-born jazz musicians.

Research for this work was sponsored in part by the Institute of Jazz Studies (IJS) at Rutgers University. The Carter-Berger-Carter Research Fellowship at IJS funded a research trip to access institute holdings on Cook and the institute's rich collection of jazz periodicals and photographs. Adriana Cuervo, Elizabeth Surles, Vinnie Pelote, Diane Biunno, and the IJS staff have my profound appreciation and thanks. Through Rutgers I also connected with photographer David Spitzer, who made photographs available from his collection for this work, including the cover photo, and I am indebted to him for his contributions.

I also would like to recognize David Gleason, webmaster and curator of the online historical library www.worldradiohistory.com. This website was a true treasure chest discovery; the site contained searchable, scanned images of most issues of *DownBeat* magazine, perhaps history's most authoritative periodical on jazz and jazz musicians. The worldradiohistory.com archive of *DownBeat* was an extraordinary reference for past album reviews, musician spotlights, and jazz record label marketing and advertising.

I am incredibly grateful for Amy Maddox, managing editor ("There is a chance!"), and to University of North Texas (UNT) Press for the opportunity to publish and make a dream a reality.

Last but certainly not least, I salute my loving family: my wife, Dr. Sabrina L. Wesley-Nero; daughter, Naomi; and son, Asa. Sabrina's love and partnership have made my life what it is. Naomi and Asa are a father's joy and both in their own ways carry forth a musical tradition in the Nero-Moore and Wesley-Montgomery families that spans generations.

Appendix 1
Discography

Herman "Junior" Cook

Chronological, by release date

1958: Kenny Burrell, *Blue Lights* (Blue Note)[1]

1958: Horace Silver, *Six Pieces of Silver* (Blue Note; combines recorded material from 1956 and 1958)

1958: Horace Silver, *Finger Poppin'* (Blue Note)

1959: Horace Silver, *Blowin' the Blues Away* (Blue Note)

1960: Horace Silver, *Horace-Scope* (Blue Note)

1960: Dave Bailey Sextet, *One Foot in the Gutter* (Epic)

1961: Horace Silver, *Doin' the Thing* (*Live at the Village Gate*) (Blue Note)

1962: Junior Cook (first recording as leader), *Junior's Cookin'* (Jazzland label)

1962: Horace Silver, *The Tokyo Blues* (Blue Note)

1962: Blue Mitchell, *The Cup Bearers* (Riverside)

1963: Horace Silver, *Silver's Serenade* (Blue Note)

1964: Blue Mitchell, *The Thing to Do* (Blue Note)

1964: Horace Silver, *Song for My Father* (Blue Note)

1965: Blue Mitchell, *Down with It!* (Blue Note)

1965: Buddy Rich, *Are You Ready for This?* (Roulette; Tokyo, 18 January 1965)

1966: Blue Mitchell, *Bring It Home to Me* (Blue Note)

1966: Blue Mitchell, *Boss Horn* (Blue Note)

1967: Barry Harris, *Luminescence!* (Prestige)

1967: Cedar Walton, *Cedar!* (Prestige)

1968: John Patton, *That Certain Feeling* (Blue Note)

1968: Don Patterson, *Opus de Don* (Prestige)

1968: Blue Mitchell, *Heads Up!* (Blue Note)

1968: George Coleman, *The George Coleman Octet* (Catalyst)

1971: Freddie Hubbard, *Sing Me a Song of Songmy* (Atlantic)

1973: Freddie Hubbard, *Keep Your Soul Together* (CTI)

1974: Freddie Hubbard, *Polar AC* (CTI)

1974: Freddie Hubbard, *High Energy* (Columbia)

1977: Junior Cook, *Pressure Cooker* (Affinity label)

1977: Mickey Tucker, *Sojourn* (Xanadu)

1977: Eddie Jefferson, *The Main Man* (Inner City)

1979: Louis Hayes–Junior Cook Quintet, featuring Woody Shaw, *Ichi-Ban* (Timeless Muse; recorded in 1976)

1979: Junior Cook, *Good Cookin'* (Muse)

1979: Louis Smith, *Prancin'* (SteepleChase)

1980: Walter Bishop Jr., *Hot House* (Muse)

1980: Mickey Tucker, *The Crawl* (Muse)

1981: Junior Cook, *Something's Cookin'* (Muse)

1981: Kenny Drew, *All the Things You Are* (All Art Promotion; recorded live in Tokyo, Japan)

1984: Clifford Jordan and Junior Cook, *Two Tenor Winner* (Criss Cross)

1984: Monky Kobayashi, *What's This: Monky Kobayashi and NY Bebop* (Paddle Wheel [Japan])

1986: *Vibration Society: The Music of Rahsaan Roland Kirk* (Stash Records)

1986: Milos Krstic, *Be-Bop Piano of Mike Krstic* (Ram [Yugoslavia])

1988: Horace Silver, *Music to Ease Your Disease* (Silverto Records)

1988: Junior Cook, *The Place to Be* (SteepleChase)

1989: McCoy Tyner Big Band, *Uptown Downtown* (Milestone; recorded live in November 1988 at the Blue Note jazz club, NYC)[2]

1989: Bill Hardman, *What's Up?* (SteepleChase)

1989: Junior Cook, *On a Misty Night* (SteepleChase)

1990: Junior Cook Quartet, George Coleman Octet, *Stablemates* (Affinity; recorded in November 1977)

1990: Larry Gales Sextet, *A Message from Monk* (Candid)

1991: Bertha Hope, *Elmo's Fire* (SteepleChase)

1991: Louis Smith, *Strike Up the Band* (SteepleChase)

1991: McCoy Tyner Big Band, *The Turning Point* (Verve)

1991: Junior Cook, *You Leave Me Breathless* (SteepleChase)

1996: Mike Longo, *New York '78* (Consolidated Artists Publishing; recorded in 1978)

1997: Clifford Jordan Big Band, *Play What You Feel* (Mapleshade; recorded in 1990 live at Condon's jazz club, NYC)

2007: Freddie Hubbard, *Freddie Hubbard Quintet: Live at Carnegie Hall, 1972* (Stepper Music; includes recordings from the quintet's performance at the Newport [RI] Jazz Festival in 1968 and the Newport Jazz Festival at Carnegie Hall, New York City, in 1972)

2008: Horace Silver, *Live at Newport '58* (Blue Note)

2009: Horace Silver, *Horace Silver Quintet: Newport Jazz Festival, 3 July 1959* (Wolfgang's Vault; both Junior Cook and Blue Mitchell solo on Silver's classic "Peace")

2009: Horace Silver, *Horace Silver Quintet: Newport Jazz Festival, 2 July 1960* (Wolfgang's Vault)

2016: Woody Shaw, Louis Hayes, *The Tour: Volume One* (HighNote Records; recording of Louis Hayes–Junior Cook Quintet, featuring Woody Shaw, live at Leiderhalle Mozartsaal, Stuttgart, Germany, 1976)

2016: Horace Silver, *Zurich 1959: Swiss Radio Days* (TCB Music)

2016: Horace Silver, *Live in Paris* (Fremeaux and Associates; recorded in 1959)

2017: Woody Shaw, Louis Hayes, *The Tour: Volume Two* (HighNote Records; recording of the Louis Hayes-Junior Cook Quintet/Louis Hayes–Woody Shaw Quintet, live from concerts in Germany and Belgium in 1976 and 1977)

2019: Louis Hayes–Junior Cook Quintet, *At Onkel Po's Carnegie Hall, Hamburg 1976* (Jazzline)

2023: Art Blakey and the Jazz Messengers, *At the Jazz Workshop 1970* (Gearbox Records; Cook featured on one track "East of the Sun," on soprano saxophone. All other tracks feature only Ramon Morris on saxophone [tenor])

Appendix 2
Legacy of Horace Silver Front Line (Horn Players)

Title	Label	Recording Date	Saxophone	Trumpet
Horace Silver and the Jazz Messengers	Blue Note (BLP 1518)	13 November 1954	Hank Mobley (tsax)	Kenny Dorham
The Jazz Messengers at the Café Bohemia, Vol. 2	Blue Note (BLP 1508)	23 November 1955	Hank Mobley	Kenny Dorham
The Jazz Messengers at the Café Bohemia, Vol. 1	Blue Note (BLP 1507)	23 November 1955	Hank Mobley	Kenny Dorham
The Jazz Messengers at the Café Bohemia, Vol. 3	Blue Note (DY-5805-01)	23 November 1955	Hank Mobley	Kenny Dorham
The Jazz Messengers	Columbia (CL 897)	5 April 1956; 4 May 1956	Hank Mobley	Donald Byrd
Silver's Blue	Epic (LN 3326)	2 July 1956	Hank Mobley	Joe Gordon
Six Pieces of Silver	Blue Note (BLP 1539)	10 November 1956	Hank Mobley	Donald Byrd

(*Continues*)

Continued

Title	Label	Recording Date	Saxophone	Trumpet
Sterling Silver	Blue Note (BN-LA 945-H)	10 November 1956	Hank Mobley	Donald Byrd
Sterling Silver		15 June 1958	Junior Cook (tsax)	Donald Byrd
		30 August 1959	Junior Cook	Blue Mitchell
		19 May 1961	Junior Cook	Blue Mitchell
		20 May 1961	Junior Cook	Blue Mitchell
		31 October 1963	Junior Cook	Blue Mitchell
		28 January 1964	Junior Cook	Blue Mitchell
The Stylings of Silver	Blue Note (BLP 1562)	8 May 1957	Hank Mobley	Art Farmer
Further Explorations	Blue Note (BLP 1589)	13 January 1958	Clifford Jordan	Art Farmer
Live at Newport '58	Blue Note (released in 2008)	6 July 1958	Junior Cook	Louis Smith
Finger Poppin'	Blue Note (BLP 4008)	31 January 1959	Junior Cook	Blue Mitchell
Blowin' the Blues Away	Blue Note (BLP 4017)	29, 30 August 1959	Junior Cook	Blue Mitchell
Horace-Scope	Blue Note (BLP 4042)	8, 9 July 1960	Junior Cook	Blue Mitchell
Doin' the Thing	Blue Note (BLP 4076)	19, 20 May 1961	Junior Cook	Blue Mitchell
The Tokyo Blues	Blue Note (BLP 4110)	13, 14 July 1962	Junior Cook	Blue Mitchell
Paris Blues	Pablo (PACD-5316-2)	6 October 1962	Junior Cook	Blue Mitchell

(*Continues*)

Continued

Title	Label	Recording Date	Saxophone	Trumpet
Silver's Serenade	Blue Note (BLP 4131)	7, 8 May 1963	Junior Cook	Blue Mitchell
Song for My Father	Blue Note (BLP 4185)	31 October 1963	Junior Cook	Blue Mitchell
		26 October 1963	Joe Henderson	Carmell Jones
Horace Silver: Live 1964	Emerald Records (EMR-1001)	6 June 1964	Joe Henderson	Carmell Jones
The Natives Are Restless Tonight	Emerald Records (EMR-CD-1003)	16 April 1965	Joe Henderson	Carmell Jones
		11, 18 February 1966	Joe Henderson	Woody Shaw
The Cape Verdean Blues	Blue Note (BLP 4220)	1, 22 October 1965	Joe Henderson	Woody Shaw
The Jody Grind	Blue Note (BLP 4250)	2 November 1966	Tyrone Washington (Muhammad Bilal Abdullah)	Woody Shaw
		23 November 1966	Tyrone Washington (Muhammad Bilal Abdullah)	Woody Shaw
Serenade to a Soul Sister	Blue Note (BLP 4277)	23 February 1968	Stanley Turrentine	Charles Tolliver
		29 March 1968	Bennie Maupin	Charles Tolliver
You Gotta Take a Little Love	Blue Note (BST 84309)	10 January 1969	Bennie Maupin	Randy Brecker

(*Continues*)

Continued

Title	Label	Recording Date	Saxophone	Trumpet
That Healin' Feelin'	Blue Note (BST 84352)	8 April 1970	George Coleman	Randy Brecker
		18 June 1970	Houston Person	Randy Brecker
Total Response	Blue Note (BST 84368)	15 November 1970, 29 January 1971	Harold Vick	Cecil Bridgewater
Horace Silver Quintet/Sextet with Vocals	Blue Note (BST 84420)	14 February 1972	Harold Vick	Cecil Bridgewater
In Pursuit of the 27th Man	Blue Note (BN-LA 054-F)	6 October 1972, 10 November 1972	Michael Brecker	Randy Brecker
It Happened in Pescara	Philology (It) W 100/101	15 July 1973	Michael Brecker	Randy Brecker
Silver 'N Brass	Blue Note (BN-L A406-G)	10 January 1975	Bob Berg	Tom Harrell
Silver 'N Woods	Blue Note (BN-L A581-G)	7 November 1975	Bob Berg	Tom Harrell
Silver 'N Voices	Blue Note (BN-LA 708-G)	24 September 1976	Bob Berg	Tom Harrell
Silver 'N Percussion	Blue Note (BN-LA 853-H)	12, 17 November 1977	Larry Schneider	Tom Harrell
Silver 'N Strings Play the Music of the Spheres	Blue Note (LWB-1033)	3, 10 November 1978; 26 October 1979; 2 November 1979	Larry Schneider (tsax, sop sax)	Tom Harrell

(*Continues*)

Continued

Title	Label	Recording Date	Saxophone	Trumpet
Guides to Growing Up	Silverto (SPR 101)	18, 19 September 1981	Eddie Harris	
Spiritualizing the Senses	Silverto (SPR 102)	19 January 1983	Eddie Harris, Ralph Moore	Bobby Shew
There's No Need to Struggle	Silverto (SPR 103)	25 August, 1 September 1983	Eddie Harris	Bobby Shew
Continuity of Spirit	Silverto (SPR 104)	25 March 1985	Buddy Collete, Don Menza, Ray Pizzi, Ernie Watts (flute)	Carl Saunders (flugelhorn)
Music to Ease Your Disease	Silverto (SPR 105)	31 March 1988	Junior Cook	Clark Terry (flugelhorn)
It's Got to Be Funky (Horace Silver Orchestra)	Legacy CK 53812	8, 9 February 1993	Eddie Harris, Branford Marsalis, Red Holloway	Oscar Brashear, Ron Stout, Bob Summers (trumpet, flugelhorn)
Pencil Packin' Papa	CBS/Sony (J) SRCS 7416	10, 11 January 1994		
The Hardbop Grandpop	Impulse IMPD-192	29 February–1 March 1996	Michael Brecker	Claudio Roditi
A Prescription for the Blues	Impulse IMPD-238	29–30 May 1997	Michael Brecker	Randy Brecker
Jazz . . . Has . . . a Sense of Humor	Verve IMPD-293	17–18 December 1998	Jimmy Greene	Ryan Kisor

Source: "Horace Silver Catalog," JazzDisco.org, accessed July 21, 2025, https://www.jazzdisco.org/horace-silver/catalog.

Endnotes

Notes for the Introduction

1. Ben Ratliff, "John Coltrane and the Essence of 1961," *Washington Post*, 7 November 2021, p. E1.
2. Bob Mondello, "Steven Sondheim Is Cool Now," *All Things Considered, National Public Radio*, 11 January 2024. https://www.npr.org/2024/01/11/1224046567/stephen-sondheim-here-we-are-merrily.
3. Ratliff, "John Coltrane."
4. LeRoi Jones, *Blues People: Negro Music in White America* (Harper Perennial, 1999), xi.

Notes for Chapter 1

1. Interview by Leigh Kamman, "Junior Cook September 1988," Leigh Kamman Legacy Project, *YouTube*, accessed 7 September 2021, https://www.youtube.com/watch?v=Pa4F42lCSmY.
2. Phone interview with Timmy Shepherd, 15 April 2022. Shepherd joked, "Junior said he would kill me if I ever told anyone his middle name!"
3. 1940 US Census, Escambia County, Florida, Pensacola, population schedule, enumeration district (ED) 17-22, page 16A, household 350, Lines 4-8, John Cook and family; digital image, Archives.gov (http://1940census.archives.gov): accessed 10 September 2025; citing NARA microfilm publication T627, roll 585.
4. 1940 US Census, Pensacola, page 23A, household 535, Lines 25-27, Aleck Echo and family.
5. Liner notes from the album *Junior's Cookin'* (Jazzland, 1960)
6. Phone conversation with Eric Cook, 2 March 2022.
7. *Pensacola News Journal*, 29 September 1946, p. 3, accessed 28 January 2023, https://www.newspapers.com/image/352816365/?terms=%22Herman%20Cook%22&match=1.
8. Leonard Feather questionnaire (hard copy) for biographic entries in his *The Encyclopedia of Jazz in the Sixties* (Horizon Press: New York, 1966). This questionnaire, completed in Cook's own handwriting, is housed in the "Junior Cook" clippings file, Institute of Jazz Studies, John Cotton Dana Library, Rutgers University, Newark, NJ (hereafter cited as Feather questionnaire).

9. 1940 US Census, Pensacola, page 16A, household 350, Lines 4-8, John Cook and family.
10. "Obituaries," *Pensacola News Journal*, 4 July 1965, p. 2, accessed 28 January 2023, https://www.newspapers.com/image/263938205/?terms=%22Herman%20Cook%22&match=1.
11. "Northwest Florida Deaths," *Pensacola News Journal*, 6 February 1975, p. 11, accessed 28 January 2023, https://www.newspapers.com/image/264784819/?terms=%22Herman%20Cook%22&match=1.
12. Noal Cohen and Michael Fitzgerald, "Rat Race Blues: The Musical Life of Gigi Gryce" (2014), page 16–17.
13. Liner notes from the album *Junior's Cookin'* (Jazzland, 1960)
14. *Polk's Pensacola* (Escambia County, FLA) *City Directory* (Richmond: R. L. Polk, 1952), 101. Digital image, MyHeritage.com (https://www.myheritage.com), accessed 10 September 2025.
15. Phone interview with Jean Jones, 10 February 2025.
16. Joe Evans and Christopher Brooks, *Follow Your Heart: Moving with the Giants of Jazz, Swing, and Rhythm and Blues* (University of Illinois Press, 2008), 21.
17. Evans and Brooks, *Follow Your Heart*, 22.
18. "*Interview with Jazz Musician Hal (Fess) Andrews,*" 3 November 1981, Florida Memory, State Library and Archives of Florida, Tallahassee (hereafter cited as Florida Memory), accessed 28 April 2023, https://www.floridamemory.com/items/show/238865.
19. Darrel Eiland, "'Children Don't Appreciate Beauty Anymore,' Says Sheppard," *Pensacola News*, 13 September 1966, p. 3, accessed 28 January 2023, https://www.newspapers.com/image/264009286/?terms=%22Herman%20Cook%22&match=1.
20. Phone interview with Joseph Herring, 6 December 2023.
21. "Interview with Jazz Musician Jimmy Cox," 5 November 1981, Florida Memory, accessed 7 December 2023, https://www.floridamemory.com/items/show/238867.
22. "*Interview with Jazz and Blues Saxophone Player John Boller," 1 December* 1981, Florida Memory, accessed 2 January 2024, https://www.floridamemory.com/items/show/238251.
23. Feather questionnaire.
24. "Interview with John Boller."
25. Herring interview.
26. "Sideman" is a common term to denote the musicians in any given group other than the leader/headliner of the group.

27. Yolanda Yvette Williams, "The Intellectual Capital of the Black Music Educators of the Twin Cities (1974–1999)" (PhD diss., University of Minnesota, April 2017), 92.
28. Noal Cohen and Michael Fitzgerald, *Rat Race Blues: The Musical Life of Gigi Gryce* (Current Research in Jazz, 2014), 17.
29. James R. McGovern, *The Emergence of a City in the Modern South: Pensacola, 1900–1945* (University of West Florida Foundation, 1976), 139.
30. Madeleine Hirsiger Carr, "Denying Hegemony: The Function and Place of Florida's Jook Joints During the Twentieth Century's First Fifty Years" (PhD diss., Florida State University, 2002), 155.
31. Jones interview.
32. Evans and Brooks, *Follow Your Heart*, 19. Historians count eight known lynchings in Escambia County, Florida (which includes Pensacola), between 1875 and 1910, including Leander Shaw, who in 1908 was dragged from a local jail and lynched from a light pole in downtown Pensacola's Plaza Ferdinand; Jennie McKeon, "Pensacola Area Lynching Victims Remembered," *WUWF 88.1*, 20 September 2018, https://www.wuwf.org/local-news/2018-09-20/pensacola-area-lynching-victims-remembered. Other instances of in-state white terrorism likely tormented Black Floridians in later decades. White mobs massacred Black residents and burned and leveled the town of Rosewood, Florida, in 1923 after a white woman claimed that a "colored man" had attacked her. In October 1934, within three months of Cook's birth, a white lynch mob tracked and followed Claude Neal, who was under police custody after being accused of the rape and murder of a white woman. The police, seeing tensions rise, transported Neal several times before the mob found Neal at a jail in Brewton, Alabama, transported him back to Marianna (Jackson County), Florida, and castrated, tortured, and lynched him in the woods on 26 October 1934.
33. "1950 Census of Population, Preliminary Counts: Population of Florida By Counties, April 1, 1950," Series PC-2, No. 9, 11 August 1950, https://www2.census.gov/library/publications/decennial/1950/pc-02/pc-2-09.pdf, accessed 22 June 2023.
34. "Duke and Ivy Feted," *Pittsburg Courier*, 11 December 1937.
35. McGovern, *Emergence of a City*, 166.
36. Cohen and Fitzgerald, *Rat Race Blues*, 26.
37. Herring interview.
38. Ben Ratliff, *Coltrane: The Story of a Sound* (Picador, 2008), 122.

39. R. D. Pierce, DeVilliers: A City Within the City of Pensacola, Florida (Author House, 2005), 37–65. "Interview with Jimmy Cox."
40. Jones interview.
41. Herring interview.
42. Jessica Forbes, "Generations of Sound: Belmont-Devilliers' Rich Musical History," *Inweekly*, 28 February 2013, pp. 9–13, https://issuu.com/inpublisher/docs/feb.28issue.
43. Pierce, *DeVilliers*, 18.
44. "Interview with Jimmy Cox."
45. John Appleyard, "Black Musicians, Singers Shaped Pensacola's Music History," *Pensacola News Journal*, 17 February 2019, https://www.pnj.com/story/news/2019/02/17/black-musicians-singers-shaped-pensacolas-music-history/2883207002/.
46. Herring interview.
47. François Postif, *Jazz Me Blues: Interviews et Portraits de Musiciens de Jazz et de Blues* (Outre Mesure, 2001), 152.
48. James Accardi, compiler, "Wardell Gray: A Discography, 1944–1955," accessed on 29 April 2022, http://wardellgray.org/discography.html.
49. Feather questionnaire.
50. Postif, *Jazz Me Blues*, 52.
51. T. Shepherd interview.
52. Liner notes for Junior Cook's *Pressure Cooker* album (Affinity, 1977), written by Brian Case.
53. Phone interview with Michael Cuscuna, 15 September 2022.
54. David H. Rosenthal, *Hard Bop: Jazz and Black Music, 1955–1965* (Oxford University Press, 1992), 23.
55. Rosenthal, *Hard Bop*, 24.
56. David Evans, *The NPR Curious Listener's Guide to Blues* (Grand Central Press, 2005), 43.
57. Email correspondence with Pensacola State College Records Support, 19 September 2022.
58. "College History," Pensacola State College website, accessed 19 September 2022, https://www.pensacolastate.edu/about-psc/college-history/#1473459288453-765b82b2-6dfa.
59. Kenneth D. Yglesias, "The Magnificent Twelve: Florida's Black Junior Colleges. Book Reviews," *Diverse: Issues in Higher Education*, 22 June 2007, accessed 21 September 2022, https://www.diverseeducation.com/institutions/community-colleges/article/15083854/the-magnificent-twelve-floridas-black-junior-colleges-book-reviews.

60. *Polk's Pensacola City Directory*, 163.
61. *Polk's Pensacola City Directory*, 190.
62. "First Came the Terror," *Washington Post*, 20 January 1985, p. F3.
63. Feather questionnaire.
64. Feather questionnaire.
65. "Junior Cook October 1985," Leigh Kamman Legacy Project, *YouTube*, accessed 28 February 2024, https://youtu.be/2MvoUdrBfdY?si=yXQk6E5aSWbqpo24.
66. "First Came the Terror."
67. Feather questionnaire.
68. Postif, *Jazz Me Blues*, 51.
69. "Junior the Elder of American Jazz," *Age Entertainment Guide*, 11 October 1991, p. 4.
70. "A Time for Silver," *Radio Free Jazz*, March 1977, p. 18.
71. Adrian Jackson, "Still Low-Key After All These Years," *Sydney Morning Herald* (Australia), 4 October 1991, p. 5S.
72. Feather questionnaire; Cook noted that he had participated in a radio broadcast with Dizzy Gillespie's combo in early 1958.
73. *DownBeat*, 18 September 1958, p. 42.
74. "Record Reviews: Kenny Burrell," "Blue Lights," *DownBeat*, 12 April 1962, p. 28.
75. "Kenny Burrell, NEA Jazz Master," interview with Anthony Brown, Smithsonian Institution National Endowment for the Arts Jazz Masters Oral History Program, 16–17 February 2010, accessed 26 April 2023, https://www.si.edu/media/NMAH/NMAH-AC0808_Burrell_Kenny_Transcript.pdf.
76. H. A. Woodfin, "Kenny Burrell: Blue Lights Volume 1," *Jazz Review*, November 1959, p. 34.

Notes for Chapter 2

1. Horace Silver introducing his new band, from *Horace Silver: Live at Newport '58* (Blue Note, released 2008).
2. "Junior Cook October 1985," Leigh Kamman Legacy Project, *YouTube*, accessed 28 February 2024, https://youtu.be/2MvoUdrBfdY?si=yXQk6E5aSWbqpo24.
3. Michael Fitzgerald, "Abart's Internationale/Abart's Jazz Mecca," *JazzMF*, April 28, 2019, https://jazzmf.com/wiki/abarts-internationale-abarts-jazz-mecca/.
4. *DownBeat*, May 16, 1957.

5. Mark Gardner, liner notes for the album *Two Tenor Winner* (Clifford Jordan—Junior Cook; Criss Cross Jazz, 1984. Leonard Feather, liner notes for the album *Finger Poppin'* (Horace Silver Quintet; Blue Note Records, 1959).
6. "Junior Cook October 1985."
7. Feather, liner notes for *Finger Poppin'*.
8. Austin Casey, "Horace Silver - Señor Blues (Horace Silver, Blue Mitchell & Junior Cook," *YouTube*, accessed 15 August 2025, https://youtu.be/t8jFGFwOm7k?feature=shared.
9. Aaron Gilbreath, *This Is: Essays on Jazz* (Outpost19, 2017), 58. Mobley's return in 1960 to the music recording studio following his incarceration led to his powerhouse Blue Note album *Soul Station*.
10. "Junior Cook October 1985."
11. Leonard Feather, liner notes to *Get Those Elephants Out'a Here* (The Mitchells: Red, Whitey, and Blue; Metro Jazz, 1959).
12. Mike Davenport, "The Jazz Scene," *Valley News* (West Lebanon, NH), 5 October 1961, p. 73.
13. Piero Scaruffi, "Hank Mobley," Scaruffi.com, accessed 19 December 2021, https://www.scaruffi.com/jazz/mobley.html.
14. Mike Falcon, "Guest Column: Review of Hank Mobley Bio," JazzCollector.com, 10 April 2011, accessed on 19 December 2021, https://jazzcollector.com/booksmagazines/guest-column-review-of-hank-mobley-bio.
15. Andrew L. Shea, "Hank Mobley: The Greatest Sax Player You Never Heard," *Spectator* (London), 6 September 2018, https://www.spectator.co.uk/article/hank-mobley-the-greatest-sax-player-you-never-heard.
16. Charles Miller, "The Life and Jazz Style of Blue Mitchell," in *African American Jazz and Rap: Social and Philosophical Examinations of Black Expressive Behavior*, ed. James L. Conyers Jr. (McFarland, 2001).
17. Barbara Gardner, "Inside the Horace Silver Quintet," *DownBeat*, 20 June 1963, pp. 20–22, accessed 10 March 2023, https://worldradiohistory.com/Archive-All-Music/DownBeat/60s/63/Down-Beat-1963-06-20.pdf.
18. Ted Gioia, *The History of Jazz*, 2nd ed. (Oxford University Press, 2011), 293. I presume that Gioia is saying that "**obsession** with virtuosity" is absent in Silver's sound, not virtuosity itself. One would quibble with Gioia's summary if it amounts to coupling virtuosity and bebop, which by his definition connotes "playing fast," and the notion that hard bop musicians were not virtuosos in their own right

because the compositions on balance were at slower tempos compared to many bebop tunes.

19. Phone interview with Michael Cuscuna, 15 September 2022.
20. Gioia, *History of Jazz*, 293.
21. *DownBeat*, 10 December 1959, p. 51, accessed 1 January 2023, https://worldradiohistory.com/Archive-All-Music/DownBeat/50s/59/Down-Beat-1959-12-10-26-25.pdf. Full-page ad for Horace Silver albums on Blue Note Records, *DownBeat*, 20 June 1963, p. 25, accessed 10 March 2023, https://worldradiohistory.com/Archive-All-Music/DownBeat/60s/63/Down-Beat-1963-06-20.pdf.
22. Shea, "Hank Mobley, the Greatest Sax Player You Never Heard."
23. Michael Cuscuna, liner notes for *Horace Silver: Live at Newport '58* (Blue Note Records, 2008).
24. Kenny Mathieson, *Cookin': Hard Bop and Soul Jazz, 1954–65* (Canongate Books, 2012), 5.
25. Duck Baker, "Horace Silver: Paris Blues," *Jazz Times*, 25 April 2019, accessed on 7 March 2022, https://jazztimes.com/archives/horace-silver-paris-blues/.
26. Bill Shoemaker, "Horace Silver: The Horace Silver Retrospective," *Jazz Times*, 1 November 1999, accessed on 7 March 2022, https://jazztimes.com/reviews/albums/horace-silver-the-horace-silver-retrospective/.
27. "In Review," *DownBeat*, 9 July 1959, p. 36, accessed 31 December 2022, https://worldradiohistory.com/Archive-All-Music/DownBeat/50s/59/Down-Beat-1959-07-09-26-14.pdf.
28. Phone interview with Valery Ponomarev, 1 September 2022.
29. "Jazz Record Buyer's Guide," *DownBeat*, 9 July 1959, p. 32, accessed 31 December 2022, https://worldradiohistory.com/Archive-All-Music/DownBeat/50s/59/Down-Beat-1959-07-09-26-14.pdf.
30. "In Review," *DownBeat*, 9 July 1959.
31. Bobby Timmons' bop hymn "Moanin'" (recorded in 1958, a year before "Sister Sadie") switches those roles, with the piano carrying the melody while the horns respond to the piano's call.
32. Ralph J. Gleason, "In Review" (review of Horace Silver's *Blowin the Blues Away*), *DownBeat*, 21 January 1960, p. 34, accessed 1 January 2023, https://worldradiohistory.com/Archive-All-Music/DownBeat/60s/60/DB%201960-01-21.pdf.
33. "In Review," *DownBeat*, 22 November 1962, p. 35, accessed 1 January 2023, https://worldradiohistory.com/Archive-All-Music/DownBeat/60s/62/DownBeat-1962-11-22.pdf.

34. Postif, *Jazz Me Blues*, 52.
35. Barbara Gardner, "Inside the Horace Silver Quintet," *DownBeat*, 20 June 1963, pp. 20–22, accessed 2 January 2023, https://worldradiohistory.com/Archive-All-Music/DownBeat/60s/63/DB%201963-06-20.pdf.
36. Richard Cook, *Blue Note Records: The Biography* (Justin, Charles, 2003), 183.
37. Cuscuna interview.
38. "Junior Cook October 1985."
39. Cuscuna interview.
40. Phone interview with Javon Jackson, 30 May 2022.
41. George Shaw, "Relationships Between Experiential Factors and Percepts of Selected Professional Musicians in the United States Who Are Adept at Jazz Improvisation" (PhD diss., University of Oklahoma, 1979), 493.
42. Bobby Watson, "Artist's Choice: Bobby Watson on Unsung New York Masters," *Jazz Times*, 25 April 2019, accessed on 7 March 2022, https://jazztimes.com/features/lists/artists-choice-bobby-watson-on-unsung-new-york-masters/.
43. Cuscuna interview.
44. "Freddie Hubbard—Jazz Master—Interview," *YouTube*, accessed 2 September 2023, https://youtu.be/jkr3_GvWmKk?si=YbIqeX_FrcJRWG1W.
45. Phone interview with Timmy Shepherd, 15 April 2022.
46. Shaw, "Relationships Between Experiential Factors," 514.
47. T. Shepherd interview.
48. Cook, *Blue Note Records*, 180.
49. "Horace Silver 5tet Tokyo Blues 1964," *YouTube*, accessed 15 August 2025, https://www.youtube.com/watch?v=eGYPzu1uODA. Barry McRae, "Joe Henderson," *Jazz Journal*, January 1969, p. 9.
50. Mark Stryker, "Junior Cook: On A Misty Night" (review), *Cadence*, July 1991, p. 73.
51. Ron Wynn, "Louis Hayes Jazz Communicators: Lou's Idea," *Jazz Times*, 1 April 2011, accessed on 14 May 2022, https://jazztimes.com/reviews/albums/louis-hayes-jazz-communicators-lous-idea.

Notes for Chapter 3

1. This review—specifically, the assertion that Cook is "content to make the changes"—reminds me of a story in Phil Woods' autobiography, *Life in E Flat*, 92: "As Gene [alto saxophonist Gene Quill] came off the stand

one night some asshole said to him, 'Gene Quill. All you're doing is imitating Charlie Parker!' Gene handed the cat his horn and said, 'Here, you imitate Charlie Parker!'" Woods, *Life in E Flat: The Autobiography of Phil Woods*, with Ted Panken, with a foreword by Bill Charlap, and with an afterword by Brian Lynch (Cymbal Press, 2020).

2. "Record Reviews," *DownBeat*, 21 Jun 1962, p. 23.
3. Mike Davenport, "The Jazz Scene," *Van Nuys (CA) News and Valley Green Sheet*, 1 February 1962, p. 117.
4. "Album Review: Junior Cook Quintet, *Junior's Cookin'*," *AllAboutJazz*, 1 March 1999, accessed 9 July 2022, https://www.allaboutjazz.com/juniors-cookin-junior-cook-fantasy-jazz-review-by-aaj-staff.
5. Phone interview with Michael Weiss, 6 July 2022.
6. Phone interview with Timmy Shepherd, 27 May 2022.
7. Email interview with Valery Ponomarev, 8 September 2022.
8. Maitland Edey, "Horace Silver: *Blowin' the Blues Away*" (album review), *Jazz Review*, March–April 1960, p. 29, accessed 14 January 2025, https://www.jazzstudiesonline.org/files/jso/resources/pdf/JREV3.3Full.pdf.
9. *DownBeat*, 5 January 1961, p. 36.
10. Carl Brauer, "Junior Cook: *Good Cookin'*," *Cadence*, December 1980, pages 53–54.
11. Bob Dawbarn, "New Records" (review of Blue Mitchell's *Down with It!*), *Melody Maker*, 4 June 1966, p. 14.
12. T. Shepherd interview.
13. Interview with Fred Daniels, 9 June 2022.
14. "Horace Silver Introduction" (track 1), on *Horace Silver, 14 February 1959: Live in Paris* (CD), (Fremeaux and Associates, 2016).
15. Liner notes for *Woody Shaw–Louis Hayes: The Tour, Volume One* (High Note Records, 2016).
16. Feather, "Herman (Junior) Cook," in *Encyclopedia of Jazz*, 100.
17. Bob Blumenthal, "Cook, Weiss Exemplify a Jazz Tradition," *Boston Globe*, 20 October 1991, p. 98.
18. "Junior Cook October 1985," Leigh Kamman Legacy Project, *YouTube*, accessed 28 February 2024, https://youtu.be/2MvoUdrBfdY?si=yXQk6E5aSWbqpo24.
19. Email interview with Patricia Landry, 18 April 2024.
20. "Junior Cook October 1985."
21. Email exchange with Berklee Archives, Berklee College of Music, 6 January 2022.

22. Alwyn Lewis and Laurie Lewis, "Richie Cole Interview," *Cadence*, September 1997, p. 19. Ed Enright, "Saxophonist Richie Cole Dies at 72," *DownBeat*, 4 May 2020, https://DownBeat.com/news/detail/saxophonist-richie-cole-dies-at-72#:~:text=In%201966%20Cole%20received%20a,Rich%20Big%20Band%20in%201969.
23. William Tesson, "Caught in the Act," *DownBeat*, 6 February 1969, p. 31.
24. "Larry Baione, 2012 November 07," interview with Fred Bouchard, Berklee Oral History Project, Archives & Special Collections, Berklee College of Music, Boston, 7 November 2012, accessed 12 June 2022, https://archives.berklee.edu/bca-011/larry-baione-2012-november-07/2012-11-07.
25. "Junior Cook October 1985."
26. Email with Landry.
27. "Jazz Program Saturday—Free," *Boston Globe*, 15 May 1968, p. 62. Edgar Driscoll Jr., "Major Attractions Posted for Boston's 'Summerthing,'" *Boston Globe*, 23 June 1968, p. 41.
28. "Freddie Hubbard: *Keep Your Soul Together*," JazzRecord.com, accessed 5 September 2022, http://www.thejazzrecord.com/records/2014/12/7/freddie-hubbard-keep-your-soul-together.
29. Pat Griffith, "Freddie Hubbard: Music Is My Purpose," *DownBeat*, December 1972, 15.
30. Robert James Lark Jr., "Selected Contemporary Jazz Trumpet Improvisations by Freddie Hubbard" (DMA diss., University of North Texas, 1994), 17.
31. Simon Hunt, "Freddie Hubbard: *Polar AC* (1975)," *Never Enough Rhodes* (blog), 13 June 2008, http://neverenoughrhodes.blogspot.com/2008/06/freddie-hubbard-polar-ac-1975.html
32. Derek Ansell, "Audio Reviews: Freddie Hubbard/Stanley Turrentine: In Concert Vols 1 and 2," *Jazz Journal*, 9 May 2019, https://jazzjournal.co.uk/2019/05/09/freddie-hubbard-stanley-turrentine-in-concert-vols-1-2/.
33. Mike Hennessey, "Rock Never Produced a Tatum, says Louis Hayes," *Black Echoes*, 28 August 1976.
34. Phone interview with Michael Cuscuna, 15 September 2022.
35. Email with Jerry Bauer, 4 December 2023.
36. Ethan Iverson, "Chronology: Paul Desmond and Ed Bickert Made Magic on *Pure Desmond*," *Jazz Times*, 8 July 2020, https://jazztimes.com/features/columns/paul-desmond-ed-bickert-made-magic-pure-desmond/.

37. "35th Annual Reader's Poll," *DownBeat*, December 1970, 17.
38. Les Tomkins interview with Freddie Hubbard, *Crescendo*, June 1973, pp. 16–18, accessed 18 April 2022, https://nationaljazzarchive.org.uk/explore/interviews/1622043-freddie-hubbard-interview-2.
39. Benny Golson and Jim Merod, *Whisper Not: The Autobiography of Benny Golson* (Temple University Press, 2016), 190.
40. Daniels interview.
41. Nathan Cobb, "There's Something New at This Year's Newport Jazz Festival. It's Called a Profit," *Boston Globe*, 7 July 1974, p. 12.
42. Freddie Hubbard Quintet, Studio 104, Maison de la Radio, Paris, March 25th, 1973 (Colorized)," *YouTube*, accessed 6 June 2023, https://youtu.be/jDWXEDaQYFk, about 19:20–19:35.
43. See Ben Ratliff's discussion of "textural music"—as distinct from earlier, more structured bop and post-bop forms—in *Coltrane*.
44. T. Shepherd interview.
45. "1975 Elvin Jones 4tet," *YouTube*, accessed 19 April 2023, https://youtu.be/CUSGcead5YI.
46. C. Gerald Fraser, "Going Out Guide," *New York Times*, 22 September 1975, p. 42.
47. "Louis Hayes Interview (2017)," interview between Louis Hayes and Maxine Gordon, WoodyShaw.com, 16 August 2017, https://woodyshaw.com/blogs/news/tour-vol-2. Phone interview with Maxine Gordon, 10 November 2023.
48. Aiden Levy, "Louis Hayes: The Master Drummer Discusses His Storied Past and Swinging Present," *Jazz Times*, November 2017, accessed online 30 May 2022, http://www.louishayes.net/LouisHayes_JazzTimes.pdf.
49. "Caught" (a regular *DownBeat* segment that summarized concert appearances), *DownBeat* magazine, 7 October 1976, pp. 39–40, accessed 3 January 2023, https://worldradiohistory.com/Archive-All-Music/DownBeat/70s/76/DB-1976-10-07.pdf.
50. Chuck Berg, "Caught," *DownBeat*, 16 December 1976, pp. 46–47.
51. "Dexter Returns," *DownBeat*, 16 December 1976, p. 11.
52. Ratliff, *Coltrane*, 152.
53. Baldur Bockhoff, "Great Jazz: Without Siemens or Sony," *Suddeutsche Zeitung* Nr. 66, 19 March 1976.
54. Maxine Gordon, in an interview with Louis Hayes published online, offered a different take, relaying that "one night in London at Ronnie Scott's Club," Cook expressed his intention to leave the band after their

tour to start a band with Blue Mitchell. After the tour ended, Cook departed and Woody Shaw recommended Rene McLean to replace Cook in the quintet, Gordon recounted; "Louis Hayes Interview (2017)" by Gordon.

55. "Concerts," *Jazz Hot*, February 1976, p. 33; "Concerts," *Jazz Hot*, March 1976, p. 35.
56. Phone interview with Louis Hayes, 16 June 2022.
57. Liner notes for *Woody Shaw–Louis Hayes: The Tour, Volume One* (High Note Records, 2016). Possibly an indirect nod to this now forty-five-year old "skirmish," both volumes one and two of *The Tour* CDs feature "Woody Shaw" and "Louis Hayes" in bold type. The CD cover photo for volume one features Cook "behind the fold"; the photo for volume two features Shaw only.
58. Steve Lake, "Woody Shaw: The Intimidator," *Melody Maker*, 2 October 1976, p. 48.
59. Chuck Berg, "Woody Shaw: Trumpet in Bloom," *DownBeat*, August 1978, p. 22. Though not referring to this band or its band members, Maxine Gordon some forty years later apocryphally wrote that there are blood families and "jazz families" and that "the jazz family has rifts and drama like all families"; Maxine Gordon, *Sophisticated Giant: The Life and Legacy of Dexter Gordon* (University of California Press, 2018), 14.
60. John S. Wilson, "Hardman-Cook Quintet," *New York Times*, 21 July 1989. *New York Times*, 8 December 1990, p. 31.
61. Email interview with Nils Winther, 2 March 2022.
62. Phone interview with Joe Farnsworth, 29 September 2022.
63. T. Shepherd interview.
64. The date of events in this anecdote was not specified. D'Rivera defected from Cuba and sought asylum at the US Embassy while on tour in Spain in 1981, according to his bio on the National Endowment for the Arts website, accessed 9 January 2023, https://www.arts.gov/honors/jazz/paquito-drivera. An early 1980s timeframe, when the Hardman–Cook quintet was in full swing and D'Rivera may have been relatively unknown in New York, is plausible. Dizzy Gillespie's management partner, Charles Fishman, relayed the outlines of such a series in *Jazz Times* (May 1992, pp. 41–42), when he spoke of presenting "Paquito at the Village Gate in three different situations," pairing him with other jazz groups.
65. "About," Jazzmobile.org, accessed 8 June 2023, http://www.jazzmobile.org/.

66. C. Gerald Fraser, "Jazz in the Streets," *New York Times*, 30 July 1976, pp. 41.
67. "Jazzmobile Begins Summer Concerts," *New York Times*, 8 July 1983, page C16.
68. T. Shepherd interview.
69. Mike Hennessey, "Bill Hardman and Junior Cook Quintet at Ronnie Scott's," *Jazz Journal*, March 1980, republished in March 2020, https://jazzjournal.co.uk/2020/03/27/jj-03-80-bill-hardman-junior-cook-quintet-at-ronnie-scotts/.
70. Email from Michael Weiss, 2 July 2022.
71. Richard Sheinin, "2021 NEA Jazz Masters: A Q&A With Henry Threadgill," *On the Corner: The SFJazz Magazine*, 15 April 2021, https://www.sfjazz.org/onthecorner/nea-qa-henry-threadgill/. "Who's Doing What, When, and Where," *New York Times*, 25 June 1982, p. C22.
72. David Wild, "News, Short Takes," *Cadence*, September 1989, p. 93.
73. Gordon, *Sophisticated Giant*, 231.
74. "JVC Jazz Festival: Coleman's Return, Salute to Gordon Disappoint," *Star-Ledger* (Newark, NJ), 1 July 1991, p. 26.
75. Email interview with Andre White, 15 February 2023.
76. "Afternoon in Jazz Button," Smithsonian National Museum of American History, accessed 15 February 2023, https://americanhistory.si.edu/collections/search/object/nmah_1420583.
77. T. Shepherd interview.
78. Phone interview with Tardo Hammer, 25 January 2023.
79. Phone interview with Ralph Moore, 19 July 2023.
80. Email interview with David Hazeltine, 28 October 2022.
81. Gioia, *History of Jazz*, 186, 197.
82. Lena Williams, "Neighborhood Report: Upper West Side; Free Music and Cheap Beer Couldn't Keep Jazz Haunt Going," *New York Times*, 28 July 1996, Section 13, p. 7.
83. Hammer interview.
84. Phone interview with Kelly Shepherd, 20 June 2022.
85. Linda Kohanov, "Music Makers Celebration Begins Tonight," *Pensacola News Journal*, 6 July 1984, p. 41. Tony Knight, "Hall of Fame," *Pensacola News*, 9 July 1984, p. 1.
86. Evans and Brooks, *Follow Your Heart*, 144.
87. Horace Silver, *Let's Get to the Nitty Gritty: The Autobiography of Horace Silver* (University of California Press, 2007), 142.
88. Phone interview with Mickey and Sheila Tucker, 25 February 2022.

89. Email interview with Roseline Hardman, 6 May 2022.
90. T. Shepherd interview.
91. Farnsworth interview.
92. Hardman interview. Phone interview with Timmy Shepherd, 22 April 2022.
93. Liner notes for the album *Two Tenor Winner*, Clifford Jordan and Junior Cook (Criss Cross Jazz, 1984).
94. Phone interview with Roberto Romeo, 9 June 2022.

Notes for Chapter 4

1. Adrian Jackson, "Still Low-Key After All These Years," *Sydney Morning Herald*, 4 October 1991, p. 5S.
2. Phone interview with Mickey and Sheila Tucker, 25 February 2022.
3. Phone interview with Don Moors, 8 October 2024.
4. Phone interview with Ralph Moore, 19 July 2023.
5. Phone interview with Timmy Shepherd, 27 May 2022.
6. Pianist Bertha Hope in late 2019 chided her interviewer, pianist Ethan Iverson, asserting that "the only people who use that word [contrafact] went to a university to learn about jazz. It's a word manufactured in a university," adding rhetorically, "Did Bach and Beethoven use the word 'contrafact'?" Iverson then asked, "Was there something you would say when the song was written on some other changes?" Hope replied, "This song is written on some other changes!" Ethan Iverson, "Interview with Bertha Hope," December 2019, https://ethaniverson.com/interview-with-bertha-hope/.
7. Phone interview with Tardo Hammer, 25 January 2023.
8. Phone interview with Michael Weiss, 6 July 2022.
9. Paul B. Matthews, "Michael Weiss Interview Part 2," *Cadence*, August 1999, page 14.
10. Ralph Moore affirmed in an interview in February 2021, "You know how Horace wrote . . . interludes, intros, tags, outros"; Coffee with Loftis, "Conversation with Ralph Moore," *YouTube*, accessed 17 July 2022, https://www.youtube.com/watch?v=Sm6FjbPCLwA.
11. Weiss interview.
12. Moore interview.
13. Phone interview with Richie Vitale, 7 February 2023.
14. Matthews, "Michael Weiss Interview Part 2."
15. Michael Weiss, entry on Organissimo jazz forum, http://www.organissimo.org/forum/index.php?/topic/33750-junior-cook/&page=2 (accessed 21 June 2022).

16. Hammer interview.
17. Email interview with David Hazeltine, 28 October 2022; Shepherd interview; Su Terry interview, 10 January 2023.
18. Hammer interview.
19. "Herman 'Junior' Cook," *The Independent* (London), 8 February 1992, p. 45.
20. Terry interview.
21. Phone interview with Joe Farnsworth, 29 September 2022.
22. Farnsworth interview.
23. Vitale interview.
24. Farnsworth interview. Phone interview with Bill Pierce, 17 February 2022. Weiss interview.
25. Terry interview.
26. Farnsworth interview.
27. Farnsworth interview.
28. Farnsworth interview.
29. "Junior Cook Shows His True Class," *The Age* (Melbourne, Australia), 23 October 1991, p. 14.
30. Dorough, a graduate of North Texas State Teachers College in 1949 (now University of North Texas), notably was the composer of the ABC television network's animated series of educational cartoons known as *Schoolhouse Rock!* Bob Dorough, National Endowment of the Arts, accessed 24 August 2024, https://www.arts.gov/honors/jazz/bob-dorough.
31. Phone interview with Kelly Shepherd, 20 June 2022.
32. Bill Milkowski, *Ode to a Tenor Titan: The Life and Times and Music of Michael Brecker* (Backbeat, 2021), 225–29.
33. Milkowski, *Ode to a Tenor Titan*, 226.
34. Moore interview.
35. Moore interview.
36. Herb Wong, liner notes for Junior Cook album *Good Cookin'* (Muse Records, 1979).
37. Zan Stewart, "Jazz Notes," *Los Angeles Times*, 20 December 1989, p. 104.
38. Tim Smith, "Junior Cook: The Place to Be" (review), *Cadence*, February 1990, p. 86.
39. Phone interview with Roberto Romeo, 9 June 2022.
40. Romeo interview.
41. Hammer interview.
42. "Junior Cook Shows His True Class," *The Age*, 23 October 1991, p. 14.

43. Tucker interview.
44. Weiss interview.
45. Hammer interview.
46. Hammer interview.
47. Hammer interview.
48. Steve Vocc, "Herman 'Junior' Cook," *The Independent*, 8 February 1992, p. 45.
49. Nils Winther, email interview, 2 March 2022.
50. Javon Jackson, phone interview, 30 May 2022.
51. Winther interview.
52. Website of Don Moors, "Artists" page, accessed 7 October 2024, http://www.donmoors.com/jc.html.
53. Phone interview with Timmy Shepherd, 15 April 2022.
54. Weiss interview.
55. Farnsworth interview.
56. Phone interview with Roberto Romeo, 23 February 2023.
57. The *Lancaster (PA) New Era*, 10 February 1992, p. 13; *Newsday* (New York), 8 February 1992; and the *Baltimore Sun*, 10 February 1992, reported that Cook died on 2 February 1992, while other press reports said that Cook died on 3 February 1992. Four outliers—the *Tampa Bay (FL) Times*, 6 February 1992, p. 27; the *LA Times*, 10 February 1992; the *New York Times*, 5 February 1992; and *DownBeat's* "Final Bar" (April 1992, p. 12)—reported that Cook was found dead on Tuesday 4 February 1992.
58. *Newsday*, 8 February 1992. The gravesite marks 3 February 1992 as the date of his death.
59. Email exchange with Doris Cook, 21 February 2025.
60. Email from Patricia Landry, 31 March 2024.
61. Farnsworth interview.

Notes for Chapter 5

1. "Junior the Elder of American Jazz," *Age Entertainment Guide*, 11 October 1991, p. 4.
2. Ratliff, *Coltrane*, x.
3. Phone interview with Ralph Lalama, 25 April 2023.
4. Phone interview with Valery Ponomarev, 1 September 2022.
5. Interview with Mickey and Sheila Tucker, 25 February 2022.
6. "Junior Cook Shows His True Class," *The Age*, 23 October 1991, p. 14.

7. "All Things You Are - Louis Hayes Junior Cook Quintet," *YouTube*, accessed 15 August 2023, https://youtu.be/9I1YwbUaR9c.
8. "Kenny Drew Quartet Featuring Junior Cook - All The Things You Are," *YouTube*, accessed 15 August 2023, https://youtu.be/2AEQfNODJbo.
9. "Bill Hardman/Junior Cook Quintet in Paris 1986," *YouTube*, accessed 15 August 2023, https://youtu.be/UA_qlBY5U60.
10. David Hazeltine, email interview, 28 October 2022.
11. Barbara Gardner, "Inside the Horace Silver Quintet," *DownBeat*, 20 June 1963, pp. 20–22, accessed 10 March 2023, https://worldradiohistory.com/Archive-All-Music/DownBeat/60s/63/Down-Beat-1963-06-20.pdf.
12. Cook, *Blue Note Records*, 180.
13. Interview with Michael Cuscuna, 15 September 2022.
14. Phone conversation with Ben Ratliff, 27 October 2023.
15. "Lakecia Benjamin Is Unstoppable," interview with Jay Metcalf, Better Sax, *YouTube*, accessed 20 August 2024, https://www.youtube.com/watch?v=GOWbeS_g_j4&t=1164s.
16. David Rosenthal, "Hard Bop and Its Critics," *Black Perspective in Music* 16, no. 1 (1988): 21–29, https://www.amherst.edu/media/view/88628/original/Rosenthal%2B-%2BHard%2BBop%2Band%2BIts%2BCritics.pdf.
17. "Jazz Recital Given by Freddie Hubbard," *New York Times*, 4 April 1970, p. 19.
18. Interview with Bill Pierce, 17 February 2022. Doug Ramsey, "On Horace Silver," *Rifftides: Doug Ramsey on Jazz and Other Matters* (blog), 19 June 2014, accessed 15 March 2023, https://www.artsjournal.com/rifftides/2014/06/on-horace-silver.html?utm_source=feedburner&utm_medium=feed&utm_campaign=Feed%3A+Rifftides+%28Rifftides%29.
19. Rosenthal, "Hard Bop and Its Critics," 29. Mathieson (*Cookin'*, 28) similarly asserts that the hard bop moniker became a "millstone" around pianist Bobby Timmons' neck, effectively typecasting him in a blues and gospel sub-category when his ability could have contributed much more to the jazz idiom as a whole.
20. Rosenthal, "Hard Bop and Its Critics," 29.
21. Ratliff, *Coltrane*, xv and xvi.
22. Cuscuna interview.
23. Interview with Ralph Moore, 19 July 2023.
24. Moore interview.

25. "Junior the Elder of American Jazz," 4.
26. Roxane Orgill, "A Sideman's Life: Whichever Way the Horns Blow," *New York Times*, 1 September 1996, Section 2, p. 24, accessed 8 January 2025, https://www.nytimes.com/1996/09/01/arts/a-sidemans-life-whichever-way-the-horns-blow.html.
27. Moore interview.

Note for Outro

1. Interview with Javon Jackson, 30 May 2022.

Notes for Appendix 1

1. Cook's sideman performance for Kenny Burrell's album *Blue Lights* was Cook's first recording for Blue Note records and possibly his first recording; liner notes for Kenny Burrell album *Blue Lights* (Blue Note, 1958).
2. YouTube footage of the big band performing in Europe, "McCoy Tyner Leverkusen October 13, 1990," *YouTube*, accessed 17 April 2023, https://www.youtube.com/watch?v=bx9VZyKdGYg.

Bibliography

Archives

Berklee Oral History Project. Archives & Special Collections, Berklee College of Music, Boston.

Florida Memory. State Library and Archives of Florida, Tallahassee.

Institute of Jazz Studies. John Cotton Dana Library, Rutgers University, Newark, New Jersey.

Newspapers. Digital Library of the University of West Florida, Pensacola. https://uwf.digital.flvc.org.

Pensacola State College, Florida.

Newspapers and Magazines

The Age (Melbourne, Australia)
The Age Entertainment Guide
AllAboutJazz
Baltimore Sun
Black Echoes
Boston Globe
Cadence
Crescendo
DownBeat
The Independent (London)
Inweekly
Jazz Hot
Jazz Journal
Jazz Review
Jazz Times
Lancaster (PA) New Era
Los Angeles Times
Melody Maker
New York Times
Newsday (New York)
On the Corner: The SFJazz Magazine
Pensacola News
Pensacola News Journal

Pittsburg Courier
Radio Free Jazz
Spectator (London)
Star-Ledger (Newark, NJ)
Sydney Morning Herald (Australia)
Tampa Bay (FL) Times
Valley News (West Lebanon, NH)
Van Nuys (CA) News and Valley Green Sheet
Washington Post

Other Sources

Carr, Madeleine Hirsiger. "Denying Hegemony: The Function and Place of Florida's Jook Joints During the Twentieth Century's First Fifty Years." PhD diss., Florida State University, 2002.

Cohen, Noal, and Michael Fitzgerald. *Rat Race Blues: The Musical Life of Gigi Gryce*. Current Research in Jazz, 2014.

Cook, Richard. *Blue Note Records: The Biography*. Justin, Charles, 2003.

Evans, David. *The NPR Curious Listener's Guide to Blues*. Grand Central Press, 2005.

Evans, Joe, and Christopher Brooks. *Follow Your Heart: Moving with the Giants of Jazz, Swing, and Rhythm and Blues*. University of Illinois Press, 2008.

Feather, Leonard. *The Encyclopedia of Jazz in the Sixties*. Horizon Press: New York, 1966.

Gilbreath, Aaron. *This Is: Essays on Jazz*. Outpost19, 2017.

Gioia, Ted. *The History of Jazz*. 2nd ed. Oxford University Press, 2011.

Golson, Benny, and Jim Merod. *Whisper Not: The Autobiography of Benny Golson*. Temple University Press, 2016.

Gordon, Maxine. *Sophisticated Giant: The Life and Legacy of Dexter Gordon*. University of California Press, 2018.

Jones, LeRoi. *Blues People: Negro Music in White America*. Harper Perennial, 1999.

Lark, Robert James, Jr. "Selected Contemporary Jazz Trumpet Improvisations by Freddie Hubbard." DMA diss., University of North Texas, 1994.

Mathieson, Kenny. *Cookin': Hard Bop and Soul Jazz, 1954–65*. Canongate Books, 2012.

McGovern, James R. *The Emergence of a City in the Modern South: Pensacola, 1900–1945*. University of West Florida Foundation, 1976.

Milkowski, Bill. *Ode to a Tenor Titan: The Life and Times and Music of Michael Brecker*. Backbeat, 2021.

Miller, Charles. "The Life and Jazz Style of Blue Mitchell." In *African American Jazz and Rap: Social and Philosophical Examinations of Black Expressive Behavior*, edited by James L. Conyers Jr. McFarland, 2001.

Pierce, R. D. *DeVilliers: A City Within the City of Pensacola, Florida*. Author House, 2005.

Postif, François. *Jazz Me Blues: Interviews et Portraits de Musiciens de Jazz et de Blues*. Outre Mesure, 2001.

Ratliff, Ben. *Coltrane: The Story of a Sound*. Picador, 2008.

Rosenthal, David. "Hard Bop and Its Critics." *Black Perspective in Music* 16, no. 1 (1988): 21–29.

Rosenthal, David H. *Hard Bop: Jazz and Black Music, 1955–1965*. Oxford University Press, 1992.

Shaw, George. "Relationships Between Experiential Factors and Percepts of Selected Professional Musicians in the United States Who Are Adept at Jazz Improvisation." PhD diss., University of Oklahoma, 1979.

Silver, Horace. *Let's Get to the Nitty Gritty: The Autobiography of Horace Silver*. University of California Press, 2007.

Williams, Yolanda Yvette. "The Intellectual Capital of the Black Music Educators of the Twin Cities (1974–1999)." PhD diss., University of Minnesota, April 2017.

Woods, Phil. Life in E Flat: *The Autobiography of Phil Woods*. With Ted Panken, with a foreword by Bill Charlap, and with an afterword by Brian Lynch. Cymbal Press, 2020.

Index

D

E

F

G

H

J

K

L

M

N

O

P

R

W

Y